TEACH YOURSELF BOOKS

ADVERTISING

This book provides an introduction to advertising and its relationship to marketing. It covers the structure of the advertising industry, its main job functions and the principles and techniques on which modern advertising is based. It also gives valuable career advice, which includes information on courses and qualifications in advertising. Each chapter contains a book list for recommended further reading.

THE AUTHOR

Eric McGregor has been in advertising since 1945, having served in a number of well-known London advertising agencies. He is currently Marketing Director of a leading pharmaceutical manufacturer. In addition to having wide practical experience, he has been closely involved in advertising education as Lecturer, Course Organiser and Examiner. Between 1966 and 1969, he was Chairman of the Advertising Association Education Committee.

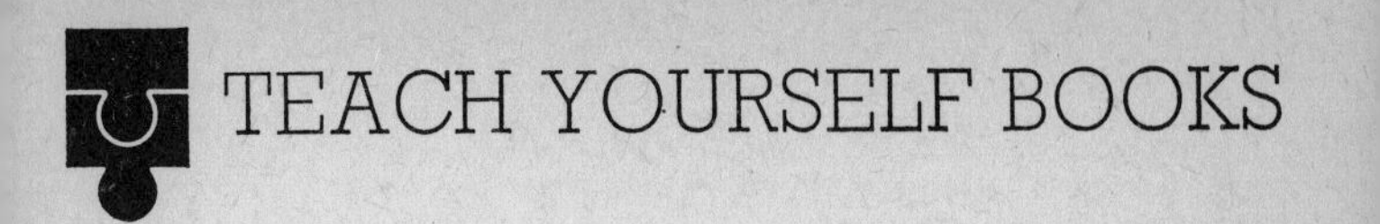

ADVERTISING

Eric McGregor

ST. PAUL'S HOUSE WARWICK LANE LONDON EC4P 4AH

First printed 1971
Second impression 1973
Third impression 1973

ISBN 0 340 15252 4

Printed in England for The English Universities Press Ltd
by Hazell Watson & Viney Ltd, Aylesbury, Bucks

Contents

Acknowledgements

The author wishes to thank all those Agencies, Companies and Organisations who have provided material which has been used to illustrate this book.

CHAPTER ONE

Advertising and Modern Society

THE FOUNDATIONS OF MODERN SOCIETY

THE last 500 years in Britain are the story of constant change. The fifteenth century brought the re-awakening of European society called the Renaissance when, after centuries of subjection to religious 'other worldliness', man began to re-explore the possibility of mastering his environment. The old order was questioned and, in the sixteenth century, successfully challenged in Britain in terms of the Reformation, scientific discovery, global exploration and the first strivings for the exercise of political power on a broader base. The seventeenth century brought further scientific and intellectual development and an extension of Parliamentary power which was ultimately to lay the foundations of democracy.

THE INDUSTRIAL REVOLUTION

However, it is in the eighteenth century that our story really begins. This is when Britain first started to become industrialised, when she put to practical use the scientific discoveries of the previous centuries and developed and extended them. The first half of the eighteenth century saw a consistent growth in mechanisation and thus of productive capacity. But it was in the second half that came the explosion which we call the Industrial Revolution.

The Industrial Revolution turned on two things: the discovery of steam power and its successful exploitation through the coal which Britain had in abundance. These factors led to an even greater expansion of mechanisation and they completely changed the character of our society.

Up to the last decades of the eighteenth century we were still predominantly an agricultural country; manufacturing was on a fairly small scale and most Britons were employed on the land. This meant that the majority lived in villages and small towns. Cities were few and far between and much smaller than they are today.

In a relatively short time we were transformed into an industrial nation. Small towns like Birmingham and Manchester expanded rapidly into major cities to accommodate not only the mushrooming factories but also the labour forces necessary to man the machines. And to the revolution in industry—*mass production*—was subsequently added the revolution in transport, namely the development of railways for the shipment of raw materials, finished goods—and people—to meet the needs of new markets, new population centres and new commercial networks.

SOCIAL PROGRESS

None of these changes was achieved without hardship and agony. The condition of the masses was appalling during the first phases of the Industrial Revolution. But out of the many horrors rose a growing awareness of the need for social justice and political liberty. There was also a growing recognition of the need for better social organisation. The systems and attitudes of Government, both national and local, suitable for the administration of an agrarian society, were totally incapable of dealing with the problems created by industrialisation and a rapidly growing population.

Thus in the nineteenth century the scope of Government began to increase enormously. Previously, its role had been confined largely to national defence and the maintenance of law and order. Now the pressures of a more complex society forced an extension of its terms of reference which would have been unthinkable to preceding generations. By the same token, however, it had to derive its power from a broader base than hitherto and the reform Acts of 1832 and 1867 progressively enfranchised every male adult in the Kingdom. The basis of a democratic society was therefore established.

Universal education followed hard on its heels. Illiteracy, although indefensible, is feasible in an agrarian society. It is untenable in an

[1] However, it was not until 1928 that *all* women were allowed the vote.

industrialised state and this was recognised formally by the Education Act of 1870, the first step in a whole series of steps which were to follow, to equip future citizens with the capacity not only to function in a modern society but also to extend their intellectual and cultural horizons.

DEVELOPMENTS IN INDUSTRY AND COMMERCE

During this time industry and commerce also changed drastically. Prior to the Industrial Revolution, most manufacture had been on a local basis. The markets served by an individual producer were therefore small and easily reached, both in terms of the provision of goods and in communicating their existence and benefits to the potential user. Mass production forced manufacturers to seek wider markets, both at home and overseas. High production necessitated high sales and these could only be achieved by wider-scale operations.

Such operations were costly. They produced the need for high capital investment, at a level frequently beyond the capacity of the family business. Thus, money had to be raised from the public and the nineteenth century saw a huge increase in share flotation. It also saw the advent of *limited liability*, since the scale of operations no longer made it possible for company management to assume *personal* financial liability if anything went wrong. All these changes altered the structure of industry. Companies got bigger and, as they did so, they began to import professional managers to help run them. One-man rule or family-rule became less and less feasible not only because of the complex problems involved but also through companies' answerability to shareholders—and indeed to the consumer.

The increased availability of goods stimulated a wide expansion in the number of outlets in which they could be bought. And the *range* of goods, which included an increasing flow of manufactures as well as of basic commodities, created a large measure of *retail specialisation.* Although the general store continued to exist in villages, it gave way in the towns to shops concentrating on the sale of particular goods: chemists; grocers; ironmongers; outfitters, etc. By the 1870s the general store had made a comeback, but this was in the form of the mammoth department store, a far cry from its humble ancestor.

Naturally, competition was severe for the rewards to be gained from growing markets deriving from a rapidly expanding population. This led, among other things, to a major development in modern commerce: the widespread *branding* (i.e., naming) of goods. It became increasingly necessary for the manufacturer to register the identity of his goods in order that they could be distinguished from those of his competitors. This was in order to protect his reputation and also to establish a basis for stimulating direct consumer demand. The process of branding goods embraced not only new products but even commodities which the consumer began to be encouraged to ask for by brand rather than by generic description.

THE DEVELOPMENT OF MODERN ADVERTISING

This is the point where advertising enters the picture, for it was in the nineteenth century that it began to be used extensively. The reason is self-evident. When manufacture was locally based and served local markets only, the need for advertising was limited. The manufacturers' goods were likely to be well-known to his immediate audience and, given also the restriction of choice which then obtained, he had no major difficulty in disposing of what he had produced.

However, as markets expanded the problems of establishing contact with an audience numbered in millions rather than hundreds forced the manufacturer to seek new methods of communication. Advertising was obviously the most convenient and cheapest way to notify potential customers who were now scattered far and wide, given that face to face confrontation (the ideal way to sell) was out of the question on grounds of utility and cost.

Newspapers were the principal vehicle for advertising. They had first been introduced in the seventeenth century and despite their high cost (due to newspaper taxes, in almost continuous operation until 1855) had grown into something like a national institution by the early nineteenth century.[1] They were, of course, the major means of disseminating news

[1] Although it was not until the 1890s that newspapers for the *masses* were introduced as the result of growing literacy.

and views broad-scale. Then as now newspapers were heavily dependent on advertising revenue; as early as the 1790s advertising agents came on the scene, who bought advertising space from newspapers, and sold it in turn, for a commission to advertisers wishing to utilise it for the promotion of their goods and services. These agents subsequently began to advise companies on how to plan and execute their advertising, and it was from this humble beginning that the modern *advertising agency* developed.

One thing quickly became evident to manufacturers; that the provision of product information alone was not enough in the context of intense competition. Many rival products were now available and it became increasingly necessary to 'sell' as well as to inform, hence the increasing use of the emotive element in advertising.

ADVERTISING AND SOCIETY

The abuses of which nineteenth century advertisers were guilty are legion and are well documented in E. S. Turner's book *The Shocking History of Advertising*. But it is also true that despite continuous social advances, there were many other abuses in nineteenth century Britain. The advertising ones are still referred to (and many people believe they still exist) while the others are now largely accepted as having been inevitable in a rough, tough society which had not fully come to terms with the need for social services, fair wages, decent housing, universal medical care and all the other elements of modern society we now take for granted. Yet advertising has come of age too, as you will see from Chapter 11.

All these social improvements underline the progress, human as well as technological, which has been made since Victorian times, which themselves were a great improvement on what had gone before. It has been a continuous story of material progress, the result of which is that *today*, in twentieth century society, the mass of people live longer, are healthier, better fed, clothed and housed than at any other time in history. Thus, although modern society brings its own problems—problems which we must solve—there is little doubt that for most people the condition of life has never been better.

Modern commerce has made a major contribution to this transformation. Mass production provides the spur of mass consumption, which stimulates broad-scale employment in order to provide the basis for achieving it. This ensures not only security for the family unit but also improved living standards, wherein advantages which were previously available only to the few can now be enjoyed by the many, including leisure and the pursuit of cultural interests as well as a wide range of material goods and benefits. Advertising has been—and is—an integral part of the whole process of development, manufacturing and selling of goods and services, a process which we now call *marketing*.

From the viewpoint of society as a whole, advertising helps to create and sustain the demand which ensures that what is produced is also consumed. It is therefore a potent factor in maintaining employment as well as consumption.

From the viewpoint of industry, advertising is a convenient and relatively inexpensive method of communication and persuasion, the most effective means yet devised for establishing contact with a mass audience.

From the viewpoint of the consumer, advertising is a service—and is largely recognised as such—in providing information which would otherwise be difficult to acquire, about the availability of goods and services over a wide area.

Advertising therefore plays an important role in the economic, commercial and social life of the country, not least in its capacity to provide the revenue for a free and independent press. It is a valuable instrument of communication for the community, bearing in mind that it is used to disseminate government information, as a major vehicle for job recruitment and for other social and cultural purposes, as well as to promote goods and services. Advertising is also extensively employed by the public itself, to buy and sell goods and houses, and in other transactions and pursuits.

In short, advertising is an indispensable factor in modern society and it would be an advantage for everyone, not only those who seek a career in it, to understand more fully its relevance to our daily lives.

FOR FURTHER READING

The Evolution of Modern Industry (F. R. J. Jervis, Harrap).
Guide to the British Economy (Peter Donaldson, Penguin Books Ltd.).
Introduction to Economics (Alec Cairncross, Butterworth & Co. Ltd.).
The Shocking History of Advertising (E. S. Turner, Penguin Books Ltd.).
Advertising in a Free Society (Harris & Seldon, Institute of Economic Affairs).
The Influences and Techniques of Modern Advertising (J. Hobson, Business Books Ltd. for I.P.A.).
What Advertising Does (I.P.A. booklet).
Advertising (Confederation of British Industry booklet).
Advertising—A General Introduction (R. S. Caplin, Business Books Ltd. for I.P.A.).

CHAPTER TWO

Marketing

THE MARKETING CONCEPT

THE Industrial Revolution was a revolution in the means of production. Although it had profound effects on *all* aspects of commerce, British industry remained for many years what is called *production oriented*. This is a mental attitude which attaches more importance to production than to the other elements of commerce.

Its origins lay in the technical advances which made it possible for a wide range of goods to be made in greater quantity and at lower unit cost than ever before. Thus the early *dynamic* in industrialisation arose from the production source and it continued to do so as newer and better machines were developed, which increased productive capacity and efficiency still further and brought even more intensive operations within reach of the manufacturer.

Parallel with this expansion in the means of providing goods there came an explosion in population and thus was created the basis for an ever-increasing demand for them. At the first population census in 1801, the British population was estimated at 9·0 million. By 1851 it had reached 16·0 million and in 1901 stood at no fewer than 41 million.[1] So, although there were periodic slumps and bankruptcies throughout the nineteenth century, in broad terms rising production and higher consumption went hand in hand.

So far as the masses were concerned, what was being produced, in the main, were the necessities of life. The purchasing power of the population at large in a low-wage economy did not permit the significant buying of luxuries. What the expanding nation urgently needed was cheap food, clothing, boots and shoes, furniture, bedding and household goods;

[1] The population in 1961 was 53 million.

these things were what manufacturers of mass-market consumer goods in the nineteenth century were chiefly in business for.

Given a virtually automatic demand for goods, therefore, it is not surprising that the 'make it first then sell it afterwards' attitude arose in industry. The major problem centred on producing basic goods at the right price. Provided it was solved, the selling task was relatively easy. If any improvements were required in the manufacturer's ability to compete, they were likely to stem from new machinery or new production methods which could fulfil the basic requirements more satisfactorily. Therefore, for many years, the chief emphasis, in terms of management-application, research, innovation and investment, was placed at the factory end of the operation.

The twentieth century has seen a steady increase in prosperity for the masses and thus of living standards. Such advances are the result both of greater political strength, arising from enfranchisement, and of higher educational standards whereby ordinary men and women nowadays will no longer allow themselves merely to work and live at subsistence level only. Coupled with this have been the progressive technological advances of this century, particularly in the last two decades, that have vastly increased not only basic output but which have also brought into being new industries and new commercial developments on a large scale, thus adding a further spur to employment and a high-wage economy. (This process has also been greatly assisted by the adoption of expansionary monetary policies since 1945.) Thus, the problem facing industry today is *no longer primarily one of producing basic necessities to utility specifications*. Most people have sufficient purchasing power to seek satisfactions which go way beyond the basic essentials of living. Indeed, their whole view of what constitutes necessities is constantly changing. Even 30 years ago, such items as cars, refrigerators and washing machines were classified as luxuries and were out of reach of most people. Now they are as much part of people's lives as furniture and bedding. So the consumer has moved on considerably from his counterpart of Victorian days. His demands cover a much broader spectrum not only in terms of quantity of goods but also in the qualities those goods must possess. To needs have been added *desires,* desires for greater comfort and convenience, for novelty and innovation, for increased opportunities for self-expression and for the enrichment of personality, to cite only a few.

In other words, the modern consumer seeks a whole range of emotional satisfactions as well as practical ones. Therefore, products have to be created which provide satisfaction at two levels: the objective and the subjective. If you doubt this, consider the importance of styling and design where furniture is concerned. Although a necessity, it is no longer something of mere utility, but an expression of the user's personality, and furniture manufacturers go to considerable lengths to accommodate the total requirements of householders, in the area of 'imagery' as well as in the provision of sound and practical goods. The same is true even where staple foods are concerned. They have to be attractively (as well as conveniently) packaged to convey an aura of quality and wholesomeness in response to the need for emotional reassurance which mothers have where the welfare of their families is concerned.

Some critics of modern commerce claim that these 'extra' requirements are largely created by commercial, and particularly by advertising, pressure. This is just not true. Without a yearning for the intangible as well as the tangible, man would never have progressed much beyond the cave. His desires go far beyond the utilitarian, hence the development of art, music, literature and other cultural activities which are not strictly 'necessary'. Commerce may capitalise on these dimensions of human nature but it does not create them—they are as old as man himself. (The difference today, however, is that nearly everyone can give practical expression to intangibles whereas in the past the opportunity to do so was limited to the few.)

What this all adds up to, therefore, is that the manufacturer today is faced with a consumer who has more power and whose demands are infinitely more complex than the nineteenth century consumer. He is also faced with a consumer whose demands can change rapidly along with the changing social scene. Today there are no 'captive' markets; no markets where needs are simple and stable and relatively easily satisfied. So the 'make it first then sell it afterwards' attitude is no longer tenable. Intense competition, the sophistication of today's consumer whose purse is long and whose demands are high, the rapidly changing pattern of needs and desires—all these rule out haphazard manufacturing and selling, especially in the context of the enormously high overheads that industry carries today.

Nowadays, no manufacturer can for long run the risk of producing goods which the consumer does not want and which will therefore be left on his hands. He has to produce them to meet the *known or anticipated desires of the consumer*, remembering again that the satisfaction the consumer requires goes far beyond what can be achieved solely on the factory floor. Thus modern commerce starts with the consumer and not with the factory. The attitude of mind and the business approach which this philosophy embodies is known as *marketing*. It is based on the concept of establishing consumer needs in advance, needs which are constantly rechecked in the light of changing social and market conditions and competitive pressures. These needs are then met in terms of an operation which takes them into account at each stage of development. Note the distinction between the *marketing concept*, the orientation towards consumer needs and desires, and the *marketing operation,* which is organising the means of satisfying them. Those who subscribe to the marketing way of life are said to be marketing oriented, in contrast to those who still cling—and there are some of them left—to the production oriented approach of the past.

MARKETING DEFINED

Here are two definitions:

> 'Marketing is the management function which organises and directs all those business activities involved in converting consumer purchasing power into effective demand for a specific product or service, and in moving the product or service to the final consumer or user so as to achieve the profit target or other objective set by a company.'
>
> (Institute of Marketing)

HOW MARKETING WORKS

PLANNING

That new product you saw in the shops today. Did you realise it was planned, meticulously and deliberately, months, probably years ago? Every single aspect of it. Marketing executives in the manufacturing company are at the centre of this planning. They co-ordinate the team of specialists whose judgement will affect the success of the operation: production managers, accountants, statisticians, packaging designers, publicity experts, and so on. Backing all this is . . .

MARKET RESEARCH

Risk is inevitable in industry. The whole enterprise turns on how well the company is able to gauge what you—the public—are going to want in the future. Big sums of money are to be invested in the product; research is vital to reduce the guesswork in this to a minimum. Research executives of many kinds must test the product itself (it's taste, price, colour, fitness for purpose—the lot!); they also test the ways in which its advantages can be best communicated to its future users, and this is tied in with . . .

ADVERTISING AGENCY CREATIVE WORK

While new products are being developed, the company's advertising agency is kept closely involved. Once the go ahead has been given, the agency's team of specialists (copywriters, artists, film producers, media planners, etc.) headed by the account executive, prepares recommendations covering the various parts of the advertising plan. These will be co-ordinated and submitted to the manufacturer's marketing manager. From there, events move swiftly to the day of the . . .

PUBLIC LAUNCH

The research stages have been completed, the advertising produced, the sales promotion schemes arranged; the agency has made its bookings with media executives in newspapers, television and so on. Now, for the first time, it reaches *you*—through advertising. The initial 'idea' has been turned into a product. Here comes the real test: will you, the customer, respond to the advertising and buy enough of the product to earn the company a profit and justify the company's risk and investment? This will depend on . . .

SELLING AND DISTRIBUTION

The manufacturer's managing director cannot now retire to the country. He can't wave a magic wand over you and make you go on buying his product, however good it is. His sales force must go on persuading and reminding multiple-store buyers and round-the-corner-shopkeepers to buy, stock, display and *sell* it to you. His distribution manager must ensure that goods are always available, so that you—the customer—can buy what you want, where and when you want it.

This is a reproduction of an Advertising Association poster, distributed through colleges and schools, which explains in simple terms, the marketing process (Reproduced by courtesy of the Advertising Association)

marketing
product research
finance
production
market research
art
copy
account group
media
merchandizing
promotion
NEW!
TAKE A LEAFLET.
retail outlet
advertising
transport
salesman
shop manager
stocks

'Marketing is the function of providing the right goods to the right people at the right time at the right cost with profit as the end result.'
(Anon.)

Both definitions are correct; longer-term you will find the first more valuable since it is all embracing. However, at this stage, the second makes the point fairly enough, bearing in mind that both emphasise the *purpose* of marketing which is basically to harmonise two things: satisfying the consumer while making an adequate profit out of so doing.

Stated like this it sounds easy, but in reality this is frequently far from the case. It is not always possible for an individual manufacturer to satisfy the consumer in a given situation *and* to make a profit at the same time.

When this incompatibility arises there is only one course of action for the manufacturer concerned: to abandon the attempt and to concentrate his efforts on other markets where the two requirements can be satisfied. This underlines the point that marketing is not an exercise in altruism but a disciplined approach to business which must always weigh the needs of the market place against the resources and skills available.

There is another important point to remember. While marketing makes extensive use of technical skills, including the growing use of the computer to process data, it is still essentially a creative process. No product proposition was ever created by the 'slide rule', although the latter can be a valuable tool in making calculations and in arriving at a better understanding of a market situation. Nor is marketing merely a matter of putting a penny into the consumer 'slot-machine' for the answers. The consumer can provide valuable indications of needs and desires, hence the vital need for continuous and skilled market research, but these can seldom if ever be crystallised in terms of actual products. It is up to the marketeer to rationalise the insights obtained from investigation and research, and convert them into dynamic product propositions.

Where new concepts are concerned, the starting point is frequently with the marketeer himself, who may anticipate a need before the consumer does. We would not have had ball-point pens, polyurethane paints, frozen foods, instant coffee and drip-dry shirts by waiting for the consumer to ask for them. Skilful marketing people, aided by advanced technology (which itself has been spurred on by the development of marketing), had to *anticipate* new needs and desires arising from changing conditions, and to express them in products and services which have transformed social, domestic and working life during the past 25 years.

THE MARKETING MIX

The marketing concept recognizes that consumer needs and desires must be satisfied in terms of the *total* proposition. This means that each element of the operation has to contribute to this process, both individually and in relation to the other elements. For example, no matter how acceptable a product may be, both objectively and subjectively, it can still fail if the price is too high, or if the advertising is badly directed or presented, or if the manufacturer fails to make it readily available in the maximum number of shops. Thus all marketing activity must be carefully co-ordinated to ensure that all requirements are met.

The elements of marketing comprise a spectrum which is known as the MARKETING MIX. These elements will vary from company to company and indeed from project to project, since both the ingredients used and the way they are blended depend upon the demands of the individual situation. The marketing mix is rather like a house. There are certain structural features which are common to all houses, but size, shape and characteristics can vary enormously in accordance with the resources, desires and needs of the individual owner.

However, let us examine those elements of the marketing mix which are common to *all* marketing operations (even though the emphasis given to each element is, of course, subject to variation).

1. *Market Research*

This is an important element in every marketing mix. Even the smallest company will want information on the markets in which it is operating, in terms of size, value, trends and competition. To this should be added information on who uses the products or services in those markets, how often they buy, where users are located and all data which enables the company to pin-point the marketing task. (See Chapter 3.)

2. *Product Development and Design*

This embraces the development and design of the product (or, in the case of a service, the development and format) which consumers within the chosen population-sector need or want, in the form which is most acceptable.

There are two things to note here. First, so far in this book we have been discussing the consumer as one entity. However, few products have universal appeal and in practical terms most products are directed at segments or sectors of the population, and thus have to be developed in line with the needs and desires of the specific audience. Secondly, note the distinction between the product itself and product design. If you use the analogy of the modern car, which is a compound of basic engineering *and* individual styling, the distinction is easy to grasp.

3. *Packaging*

Packaging is an integral part of most propositions, not only because of its utility (utility is important, i.e., packaging must be convenient and practical) but also through its potential capacity to enhance the value of the product. While this is true in all markets, the point can best be emphasised by reference to cigarettes and cosmetics, where packaging in terms of design, styling and colour is of particular importance, indeed a major dynamic in influencing brand selection.

4. *Distribution*

Each company has to arrange for its products and services to be made available to prospective users. This is known as *distribution*; in marketing the word is used to describe the process of selling to the wholesale and retail trades rather than the physical warehousing and transportation of goods (although, of course, this is an important part of the total operation). Thus a manufacturer of packaged foods will take the necessary steps to distribute (i.e., sell) them to the grocery trade so that they are available to the housewife in supermarkets and food shops up and down the country; similarly, a tour operator will make arrangements to ensure that his packaged holidays are offered for sale through travel agencies.

To effect the distribution task, manufacturers and sponsors of services employ sales forces, whose job it is to make contact with trade buyers to inform them and to persuade them to stock and sell their goods and services. Clearly, this is a vital task since the whole chain of marketing is broken if distribution of goods and services is faulty or inadequate. Timing is important. Distribution must be optimised *before* the consumer advertising breaks, otherwise demand will be created for something the consumer may find it difficult or impossible to obtain, which is both wasteful and damaging.

In some cases distribution is effected direct to the consumer instead of through retail channels. Mail order is a typical example, but in recent years there has been significant growth in personalized selling operations to the public such as those of the Avon Cosmetic Company. In the latter case, sales forces are employed similar to those of other manufacturers except that instead of selling to the trade they are in face-to-face confrontation with members of the public.

5. *Advertising*

This is a basic element in almost every marketing mix bearing in mind that even with small companies advertising is frequently used to promote goods and services to trade buyers even if their budgets do not permit advertising to the public. As a means of disseminating information advertising is indispensable to most companies, although, of course, to those who use it on any significant scale it can play a vital role in the whole process of *stimulating demand.*

6. *Sales Promotion*

As with advertising, there are very few companies who omit promotional activity from the marketing mix. Promotions can range from elaborate devices as used by—say—petrol companies down to simple price cutting in the local store, and most manufacturers and sponsors of services will make some use of them in a given marketing operation. (See Chapter 9.)

7. *After-Sales Service*

This is a vital element in the marketing mix for manufacturers—and retailers—concerned with durables such as cars, refrigerators, washing machines and equipment generally. But it is often overlooked that nearly *every* manufacturer makes some provision to provide an after-sales service, if only to deal with complaints. A crucial element in marketing is to ensure *continued* consumer satisfaction and the existence of after-sales service is an important contribution to this process.

The marketing mix is a compound. It embodies far more than production and sales—or for that matter advertising. All elements are important, but it should be constantly borne in mind that their *relative* importance in a given marketing situation varies with the nature of the product, the nature of the market and the nature of the competition.

With some projects, advertising may be of major importance (particularly in mass consumer markets) and thus the emphasis given to it in the marketing plan, in terms of expenditure and effort, will be correspondingly significant. With other projects (e.g., in the industrial area) it may be *relatively* less important and thus it will receive less emphasis than—say—the selling activity. There are no hard and fast rules; the decisions which are taken depend upon the circumstances prevailing.

One final point. All elements in the marketing mix interact on one another. For example, bad advertising will retard the progress of an otherwise good proposition. Conversely, good advertising will not support a bad proposition for long. The advertising may induce trial purchase, but the product will not be bought again if it fails to give satisfaction. This underlines once again the *totality* of modern marketing.

FOR FURTHER READING

Basis for Marketing Decision (L. Cheskin, Business Publications Ltd.).
Marketing and Market Assessment (J. L. Sewell, Routledge & Kegan Paul Ltd.).
Marketing (Colin McIver, Business Books Ltd. for I.P.A.).
Marketing in a Competitive Economy (L. W. Rodger, Hutchinson Publishing Group Ltd.).
Marketing Guide Book (I.P.A. publication).
Marketing Check List (I.P.A. publication).

CHAPTER THREE

Market Research

MARKET RESEARCH

MARKET research is used extensively today to provide information to assist the process of decision making in marketing. Its value is becoming increasingly recognised but, at the same time, it should be borne in mind that research is a tool and not a substitute for judgement. Used properly, however, it can reduce the margin of error, sometimes quite substantially. There are basically two kinds of research:

(i) Desk research.
(ii) Field Research.

Desk Research

This is the collection and analysis of *published* information derived from Government sources, trade associations and commercial companies specialising in the provision of data. Such information covers a wide range: production figures; export/import data; retail distribution patterns; population size, breakdowns and trends; consumer spending; advertising expenditure etc. Government publications such as the Monthly[1] Digest of Statistics, the Censuses of *Population, Production* and *Distribution* and the *National Income and Expenditure Blue Book* play an important part in desk research. However, commercially sponsored publications such as the *Economist Intelligence Unit Reports* are also of great value. Another source of important information, that relating to advertising expenditure, is the monthly report published by *Media Expenditure Analysis Ltd* (MEAL).

Desk research is essentially an activity designed to provide general background information and is the starting point for all market analyses. However, it can seldom throw light on what is happening to specific

[1] Also published on yearly basis as the *Annual Abstract of Statistics.*

brands, i.e., who buys them, what they think of them, etc. No published statistics could possibly cover individual commercial operations in this depth, and such information can be obtained only by conducting specifically commissioned research.

Field Research

This is a generic description and not a method of research. It simply means 'going out to find out' as distinct from getting information from published sources. At this point, the manufacturer or investigator is engaged in market research proper.

SURVEYS

Now all market research is based on the precept that it is not necessary to interview the UNIVERSE, that is to say the entire population or everyone in a given population sector. Instead, a small percentage, known as the SAMPLE, can be interviewed. Provided the sample is representative of the given Universe, in terms of age, sex, class, location and any other control relevant to the survey (e.g., those with or without children), the answers it gives will represent those of the total number of people within this universe. This is the principle on which the well-known political Opinion Polls operate and provided it is implemented correctly, it works within a predictable margin of error (usually 2%–3%). An investigation carried out among people which is based upon this principle is called a SURVEY. It is usually designed to establish what people do in a given situation (what products/brands they use, when they use them, etc.). A survey is a *quantitative* exercise, that is to say its purpose is normally to produce information which can be expressed statistically. There are three ways of selecting a sample.

Random Sample

This is based on the principle that every member of the Universe should have an *equal* chance of being interviewed. Where the general population is concerned, the electoral register is the usual source from which the sample[1] is drawn, since it gives the names and addresses of all voters district by district. The names of the people to be interviewed are selected at random. Interviewers must then ensure that there is no deviation from the sample. If qualifying respondents are not at home or not available, the interviewer must call back, if necessary time and time again in order to maintain the random nature of the sample. Naturally random sampling is very expensive and it can be time consuming, so although it is the ideal method it is less often used.

Quota Sampling

This method is more commonly used. It is based upon giving interviewers a quota of respondents to interview (e.g., 30 men in A–B class aged 45 or over). It is then up to them to ensure they select respondents who qualify. Naturally, this involves judgement on the part of the interviewers, although trained interviewers seldom interview the wrong people. (In all surveys, regardless of the sampling method used, anything up to 10% of all respondents are re-contacted by the company carrying out the research to make certain that the interview really has taken place and that the respondent qualifies.) However, while this method can provide a sample accurate in terms of basic characteristics used to structure it (e.g., so many people by sex, age and class) it may be wrong in its proportions of other characteristics. For example, young men may either have traditional views or be 'way-out', yet all will fit the quota description. Nevertheless, because of the convenience, lower cost and relatively faster output, the quota method is widely employed, bearing in mind that research investigators are very experienced in pin-pointing the prospects needed for interviewing.

Panels

These are groups of people who are recruited on a semi-permanent basis to provide continuous information over a period of time. This is in

[1] A total list of respondents from which any sample is drawn up is called a *Sampling Frame*.

contrast to the two previous methods, where respondents are selected for a one-off survey. The advantage of obtaining continuous information is, of course, that changes can be recorded and trend data plotted. A common use of panels is by research companies who specialise in recruiting housewives, whose purchases are regularly recorded either through diary-entries made by the housewives themselves, or by a physical check on their pantries made by an investigator. The disadvantage of the panel method is that information being recorded regularly tends to make the respondent *conditioned* and thus she may become atypical. To overcome this members of the panel are eliminated and replaced by new panel-members every so often.

The panel method is also used to audit (i.e., measure) sales into and sales out of retail outlets. Indeed, it was originally evolved for this purpose. One of the leading companies in this field is the *A. C. Nielsen Company Ltd.*, which pioneered this method of research as long ago as 1923. Nielsen audits cover chemists, grocers and confectioners, the three main fast-moving packaged goods markets in Britain; they are a major source of data relating to market size and trends, competitive sales and brand shares.

One note about sample sizes. Clearly the larger the size, the more precise the information is likely to be. However, even a small sample can provide reasonable indications if it is representative. The decision on sample size depends upon the breakdowns of respondents necessary, the degree of precision required and, of course, the cost. It should be remembered that increasing the sample size does not necessarily increase the precision *pro rata* (e.g., a sample size which is doubled does not give 100% greater precision).

Planning a Survey

There are four basic problems to solve in carrying out a survey:

(i) defining the objectives with precision
(ii) choosing the right sample
(iii) asking the right questions
(iv) proper interpretation of the results.

At the outset, it is of crucial importance to pre-determine what the *objectives* of the survey are. Failure to do this often means that information is obtained which cannot be used.

Choosing the *correct sample* is also vital, for everything turns on interviewing people who are truly representative of the Universe. A classic example of selecting the wrong sample was in the survey carried out by an American magazine in 1936. It was a publication read mainly by wealthy businessmen who were opposed to the then policies of President Roosevelt. A survey was mounted among its readers, seeking information on which Presidential candidate was preferred in the elections being held later that year. Not surprisingly, most of the readers interviewed plumped for Roosevelt's opponent and, on this basis, the magazine predicted a crushing defeat for Roosevelt. In the event, the latter was elected by a sweeping majority and the magazine went out of business. The reason for the wrong prediction was, of course, that the survey was not representative of the entire population but only of a section of it. An elementary error which is seldom made today but one which demonstrates the importance of making sure that those interviewed or questioned in a survey are a microcosm of the whole. This generally means that all relevant classes and ages and a proportionate breakdown of the sexes must be included in the sample.

The problems involved in asking the right *questions* are too specialised to be dealt with here in great detail. The important points to be remembered are:

(i) It is vital to avoid 'leading' questions; e.g., the question should never be asked 'how much tea do you drink?' before establishing whether or not the respondent drinks tea.

(ii) Questions must be unambiguous, that is they should be readily understood by, and mean the same thing to, all respondents. (In every survey a *pilot survey* is undertaken to check whether the questions are capable of providing the information required.)

It need hardly be said that great skill and care has to be taken to ensure *objective* interpretation. In research there is nothing the marketeer likes better than 'tidy' results and the temptation is always present to ignore or overlook those indications which spoil an otherwise neat pattern of response. Yet human beings are seldom tidy in the way they live and do things, and variations in behaviour which are revealed in survey answers can reflect very significant characteristics within the universe. For example, where shaving is concerned, electric razor users can and do use wet shaving methods as well and proper delineation of this fact could be highly important to a manufacturer in either category.

MOTIVATION RESEARCH

To establish what people do is clearly important. However, it is also important to establish *why* they do it (e.g., why they choose certain brands and not others, etc.). For information designed to gauge *attitudes* (as distinct from obtaining purely factual information) it is necessary to undertake motivation research.

It is essentially a *qualitative* exercise, one which is sometimes but not always supervised by a psychologist. It is, by definition, designed to *explore* the less tangible areas of consumer behaviour and therefore the use of the straight question-answer technique is neither appropriate nor feasible. However, it can establish *hypotheses* which may be developed and quantified subsequently by a statistical survey.

In motivation research it is not necessary to interview large numbers of people. The attitudes of a relatively small number of people should be sufficient. Samples, therefore, are quite small; while they should reflect as far as possible the characteristics of the Universe, they can never be representative in strict market research terms because of size limitations. It may be asked how information derived from such a limited number of respondents can be reliable. The answer is that the researcher is seeking *insights* rather than facts. Experience has shown that, when attitudes emerge *strongly* enough from such research activity, they are likely, on probability, to be held by significant numbers of the wider population (although, of course, where major decisions are required it is desirable to validate such results by quantitative research).

The two most common methods of conducting motivation research are *group discussions* and *depth interviews*.

Group Discussions

Groups of people, usually about 8–10 in number, are gathered in a central place and, under a group head (a psychologist or experienced motivation researcher), are encouraged to discuss a given subject. The people concerned are, of course, told they are participating in a commercial research project, but they do not know at the recruitment stage the precise context in which their opinions and attitudes are being sought. This is to prevent the group becoming conditioned and to ensure that viewpoints are spontaneous as far as possible. No questionnaire is involved,[1] the group leader relying on a private check list of (predetermined) subjects to be covered. It is his job to guide the ensuing discussion so that it is relevant yet wide-ranging, and also to ensure that everyone is given the chance to speak (it is important to prevent the discussion from being dominated by one or two people).

The advantage of the group discussion method is that it is essentially dynamic, that is it encourages interchange of ideas and experiences not possible with the individual on his or her own. Its disadvantage is that, even in this frank age in which we live, there are certain subjects or attitudes which consumers are reluctant to talk about in public, or on which they find it difficult to be articulate.

Depth Interviews

This is similar to the above except that it centres on discussion with *individuals*. Thus the researcher is encouraging one person to talk, with no one else present, instead of stimulating a group of people to talk. Otherwise the principle is the same. The advantage of the depth interview is that it can reveal insights into those consumer attitudes where the problems are subtle, or the subject-matter is intimate, which would not be so readily gauged in group discussions. In other words, it is capable of providing information in greater depth. Its disadvantage is that the group dynamic is missing and the respondent can overlook those things in

[1] This is called *unstructured* interviewing; where questionnaires are used, as in the survey, the description applied is *structured* interviewing.

private discussion which he or she would be reminded about from the contributions of others.

From the advantages and disadvantages of both methods you will see that, on occasions, it is desirable to use them complementarily and such procedure is in fact quite common.

PRODUCT RESEARCH

A considerable amount of research is carried out which covers the exposure to the consumer of specific products. A manufacturer may wish to get consumer reactions to a new product before he commits himself to extended production, or to an existing product to explore possible avenues for improvement, or competitive products to gauge their strengths and weaknesses.

A widely used method is the *placement test.* A sample of consumers is recruited and invited to try the product, quite often in the home. (The duration of an in-home trial depends upon the usage-pattern of the product, e.g., with a toothpaste used daily a test period of 14 days or even 7 days is adequate.) It is common for other products to be used for 'control' purposes, e.g., when the manufacturer wants to obtain *comparative* reactions. Thus, if he wishes to test a new version of his product, he may include in the test the existing product and possibly competitive products in order to gauge comparative consumer preferences. At this stage 'blind' testing is often employed, that is to say the products are specially packaged in blank containers and cartons in the test. (This is because brand names can bias the consumer's reaction.) At the end of the test, the user is asked for his/her views on the products tried, which are transmitted via a written questionnaire. By this means the manufacturer obtains a reasonably *objective* consumer evaluation of his product.

If it is favourable the manufacturer can at least be assured that his product is potentially acceptable in terms of its basic characteristics. (Note: in the case of blind testing of a *new* product it will also, of course, be necessary to test different name-combinations on groups of consumers to establish which name is likely to be most acceptable.)

PACK TESTING

Packaging plays a major part in the total proposition, and when manufacturers are introducing new products tests are carried out to gauge reactions to alternative pack designs, the purpose being to establish the design preferred in relation to the product itself, the image conveyed by the pack and its impact at point of sale. (Such tests are also undertaken when manufacturers wish to change the pack design for an *existing* product.) A number of methods are employed ranging from group discussions to actual in-store testing, all of which involve the exposure of pack designs to groups of consumers generally representative of the universe for the market in which the proposition is to be or is being sold.

TEST MARKETING

Much of the market research activity discussed so far is a *prelude* to action in the market place, which is carried out to provide guidance on the policies to be adopted. Thus it embraces study of what consumers have done, what are they doing and even why. All of this is very valuable, since in any situation the sensible manufacturer will seek to maximise his knowledge of a given market before he commits expenditure and effort therein. However, even the most extensive information will not provide any guarantee that the action he takes will be successful (although it should certainly help to reduce risks). Therefore, if for an existing product his proposed marketing plan embodies a significant change on previous policy (e.g., a change in packaging or price, a major alteration in advertising weight or message, or a new method of promotion), he will frequently carry out a test marketing operation. Such an operation is highly desirable, indeed even more so where a *new* product is concerned.

One of London's leading marketing experts, Stanley Pollitt, has defined *test marketing* as 'experiments set up to measure the effects of selling to consumers through normal channels'. Thus, it is a *live* test under actual market-place conditions, as distinct from other types of research (although, of course it is still essentially a research activity). The essence of the task is to minimize the risk of national or even large-scale regional marketing by studying a product's performance on a small scale, with limited investment. The assessment which has to be made is whether the proposition, and the plan created for it, stand up to the realities of the market place.

Test marketing employs the same principle as other types of research. Just as in those a relatively small number of people are chosen to represent a much larger group, so in test marketing a *region* is selected to represent the country as a whole. (Towns are sometimes used; usually, however, town testing is a preliminary stage and is followed by regional testing.)

The advantages of test marketing are obvious. The manufacturer is able to gain valuable operational experience over a wide spectrum of activity without incurring either the *costs* of national marketing or its *risks* should his proposition prove faulty (i.e., the deficiency is limited to a region instead of being exposed nationally).

The disadvantages are that no one region of the country is fully representative of the nation as a whole. There are wide regional variations in consumer behaviour, particularly in certain product categories such as soup, biscuits, cereals and medicines (this is why dual-test markets are sometimes mounted, e.g., a northern v southern operation). Moreover, the tempo of some markets is such that many of the lessons learned over the duration of the test (usually 6 months to a year is necessary) may not be fully applicable at national marketing stage. Even in more stable markets, the national situation will probably still be different from the conditions of the regional test market because of competitive activity (e.g., the introduction of competitive new products nationally while the test was running), quite apart from changes in the economy and other factors which introduce new variables. Also, of course, test marketing informs competitors of a company's intentions and this can lead to retailiatory or defensive action on their part. Thus even a test market is not an infallible guide to what may happen nationally. Nevertheless, it can provide valuable insights, provided the manufacturer takes into account the variables referred to and, of course, provided he measures the results accurately and objectively. These last will relate to trade and consumer acceptance, the latter being the ultimate criterion of success or failure. And by acceptance is meant *re-purchase* as distinct from *trial purchase.* In other words, having bought the new proposition once, are a sufficient percentage of consumers satisfied enough to buy it again? If not it is deficient and must be improved or withdrawn. Such information is obtained by the employment of consumer research (*ad hoc* surveys or panels). Another desirable research activity in test marketing is retail auditing, to measure trade acceptance and sales into and across the counter.

FOR FURTHER READING

Principles of Market Research (A. H. R. Delens, Lockwood & Son Ltd.).
Modern Market Research (M. K. Adler, Lockwood & Son Ltd.).
Motivation Research (Harry Henry, Lockwood & Son Ltd.).
Motivation Research in Advertising and Marketing (G. H. Smith, McGraw-Hill Publishing Co. Ltd.).

CHAPTER FOUR

The Advertising Industry

ADVERTISING AND PROMOTION EXPENDITURE

ALTHOUGH advertising is only a part of the marketing mix, it is a very important part, and in terms of the scale of its operations and the expenditure involved it merits the description of *industry*.

In 1971, approximately £591 million was spent in Great Britain on advertising, a sum equivalent to 1·2% of the Gross National Product. This relates only to what is called *media* or *above the line advertising* (in press, television, posters, etc.). No reliable information is available for 1971 expenditure on *sales promotion* or *below the line* activity (exhibitions, display material, circulars, money-off vouchers, etc.), but it is likely to have been at the £350 million level.

THE ADVERTISING INDUSTRY

The industry is made up of four groups, with each group involved wholly or in part with advertising operations. These are:

1. The Advertisers
2. The Advertising Agencies
3. Media Owners
4. Ancillary Services.

1. *The Advertisers*

Most companies of any significance advertise their products or services, even if only to specialist audiences. Thus the *Advertising Department* is a common feature of the commercial scene. Its size varies with the extent of a company's activities. It can range from a full scale unit of 80 or more down to one man. At its head is the *Advertising Manager* (sometimes called the *Publicity Manager*), who is usually responsible to marketing management but occasionally to sales management.

The functions of the Advertising Department are to:

formulate and implement advertising policy within the framework of marketing policy;

administer press, television, radio and poster advertising (as applicable);

create, produce and distribute display material, brochures, catalogues, labels and ancilliary material in general;

organise and control exhibitions and other sales promotion activity (including press and public relations if the company does not employ a P.R.O.).

The Advertising Manager must be fully experienced in advertising and be able to evaluate creative work (i.e., the advertising message). He must also understand advertising agency structure and procedures in order to advise on the appointment of an agency and to be able to get the best work and service from it.

Apart from the Advertising Manager and *supporting executives,* many big companies and also companies with specialised operations (e.g., department stores, pharmaceutical manufactures) employ advertising personnel in the creative, media and other areas and are thus staffed very much like advertising agencies. Such personnel may be used to create advertising or to evaluate an agency's proposals or to bring specialist skills into certain aspects of company operations which the normal agency may find it difficult or unprofitable to cover.

In recent years a different system of advertising control has been developed and is now in operation in a number of companies. This is the *Brand Manager* system, wherein executives are appointed to look after *all* aspects of marketing, *including advertising,* for a brand or brands. This means first that advertising operations are potentially even more closely integrated with marketing. Secondly, that the title of Advertising Manager is then abolished (although the *Advertising Services Manager* can exist; his function is to provide services to Brand Managers). Brand Managers are, of course, part of marketing management. In bigger companies they are answerable to *Group Brand Managers* (who control a number of brands via Brand Managers) who in turn are responsible to the *Marketing Manager* (who has ultimate responsibility for all brands). In medium sized companies the Brand Managers usually report direct to the Marketing Manager.

The Advertising Manager or the Brand Manager (the latter must, of course, have specific experience in advertising) are the main links between the advertiser and its advertising agency. They must interpret the company's marketing policy to the agency and brief it on the development of advertising strategy. To this end they work closely with the agency's account (i.e., client) management team, and where necessary, other agency personnel.

2. *The Advertising Agencies*

There are more than 600 agencies in Great Britain. The most important of them are members of the *Institute of Practitioners in Advertising,* a professional body which regulates agency practice. I.P.A. agencies account for 90% of all turnover through agencies and in total employ some 15,600 people (as at September 1971) including secretarial and clerical staff.

Agencies vary enormously in size from £23 million billing[1] with staff of 1,000, down to £100,000 billing with ten employees or so. Many, of course, are members of international groups, with total world-wide billings of hundreds of millions of dollars. Regardless of size, however, agencies have the same basic responsibilities to their clients.

Their prime responsibility is, of course, to plan and implement advertising and promotion campaigns directed at users of products and services to persuade them to use those of their clients. In order to discharge it, agencies have to participate in a wide range of activities. Thus the service they offer is broad in scope. They must first analyse in depth the products or services to be advertised; their quality and performance, their pricing and advantages over competition. This is followed by a thorough analysis of the markets in which they can be sold. Only then can agencies propose the media to be employed and the right kind of

[1] Billing means billing of clients' budgets.

advertising message. Frequently, however, their recommendations cover packaging, distribution and other elements of the marketing mix and may even embrace proposals for product improvement before the plan is put into operation. When the plan is agreed, investigation and research at each stage is undertaken or initiated by agencies to ensure that the objectives are being met.

The pivot of the agency operation is account management. *Account Executives* are the key co-ordinators; they work closely with the client's advertising or brand manager, receive and transmit briefs and ensure that all plans are progressed correctly and on schedule. Although generally regarded as administrators (they must certainly be good at administration), Account Executives frequently have a major voice in policy and many of them are experienced not only in advertising but also in marketing generally.

Agencies employ a wide range of specialists[1] covering: market research, market analysis and marketing, media planning and buying and advertisement creation (copywriting, script writing, visualising and art direction). Thus account management has in support a number of skilled personnel and wide resources to tackle and solve problems which usually go far beyond the 'slogans' of popular mythology. An agency needs *creative talent* among its writers, artists and film producers to project its clients' brands meaningfully and memorably; *planning skills* to select the right markets to attack and to deliver the best means of reaching them; *contacts* with newspapers and television studios to ensure that clients' advertisements are placed and displayed to the best advantage;

[1] Smaller agencies, of course, may have to employ certain specialists on a freelance basis rather than retain them on their permanent pay roll.

This diagram shows the full range of services which a modern advertising agency offers. In a large agency such services are an integral part of its operations; smaller agencies may find it necessary to purchase some of these services from outside companies or consultants

(Reproduced by courtesy of Institute of Practitioners in Advertising)

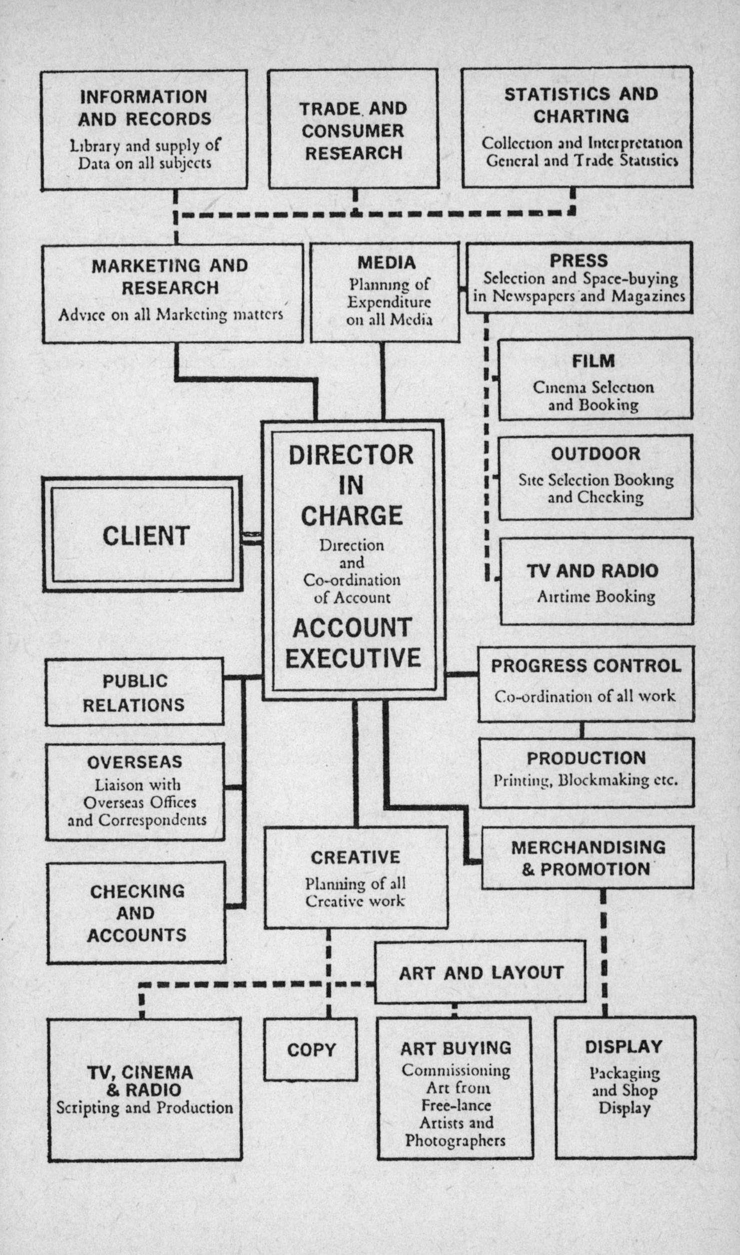
INFORMATION AND RECORDS
Library and supply of Data on all subjects
TRADE AND CONSUMER RESEARCH
STATISTICS AND CHARTING
Collection and Interpretation General and Trade Statistics
MARKETING AND RESEARCH
Advice on all Marketing matters
MEDIA
Planning of Expenditure on all Media
PRESS
Selection and Space-buying in Newspapers and Magazines
FILM
Cinema Selection and Booking
OUTDOOR
Site Selection Booking and Checking
TV AND RADIO
Airtime Booking
CLIENT
DIRECTOR IN CHARGE
Direction and Co-ordination of Account
ACCOUNT EXECUTIVE
PUBLIC RELATIONS
OVERSEAS
Liaison with Overseas Offices and Correspondents
CHECKING AND ACCOUNTS
PROGRESS CONTROL
Co-ordination of all work
PRODUCTION
Printing, Blockmaking etc.
MERCHANDISING & PROMOTION
CREATIVE
Planning of all Creative work
ART AND LAYOUT
TV, CINEMA & RADIO
Scripting and Production
COPY
ART BUYING
Commissioning Art from Free-lance Artists and Photographers
DISPLAY
Packaging and Shop Display

efficient personnel and procedures to provide a quick-off-the-mark service for clients.

Agencies derive about 75% of their income from commissions they receive from media owners with whom they place advertisements. The remaining 25% is derived from fees for special tasks, such as marketing, research, advice and planning for new product development, and from other assignments, which can even include planning of clients' sales conferences. Many agencies are general agencies, that is they are equipped to take on most business. Some, however, specialise in industrial, technical, classified or financial advertising. The principles of operation are similar in all cases.

3. *Media Owners*

The advertising message can be delivered by many different means. Newspapers, magazines, television, cinema and posters are the principal vehicles but other outlets for advertising can be used. All are known as *media.*

Media organisations have a dual-selling task. (i) They have to attract advertising revenue from companies and agencies. Consequently, they have to advertise and promote these media in all areas where space and time buying decisions are made and influenced. (ii) They have to ensure that they can deliver appropriate readership or viewership for given media, thus it is necessary to promote such media to the public. (Media owners are big advertisers themselves.)

At the centre of these operations is the *Advertisement Manager.* His title is perhaps misleading since he is responsible for the sale of space and indeed in some media organisations he is now known as *Sales Manager,* for this is really what he is. He has under his command, representatives or sales executives whose task it is to call upon advertisers and agencies and sell them on the merits of the media under his control. This used to be a 'slap 'em on the back job' but it is far removed from that nowadays. The sophistication of media planning and buying today forces the media organisation and thus the representative to use a sophisticated selling approach, frequently geared to a specific advertising problem of the advertiser or agency. Media organisations undertake considerable research to establish both qualitative and quantitative data about the media they control in order to demonstrate their effectiveness as vehicles for advertising. While such research is a selling tool, it is also a valuable service to advertisers and agencies since it supplements industry media research operations.

In addition to supervising face-to-face selling, the Advertisement Manager must initiate advertising campaigns to prospective buyers of space or time. These may be both planned and implemented under his auspices; in some cases, however, the implementation may be delegated to advertising executives within the organisation.

Such campaigns embody the extensive use of brochures and rate cards as well as advertising in professional and trade journals. Their chief characteristic is the provision of factual information; space and time buying is a business activity and the customer requires facts rather than hyperbole. Considerable ingenuity is wanted, and often displayed, in projecting facts in an interesting, indeed dramatic, way bearing in mind that the advertiser in these cases is addressing a professional audience.

The Advertisement Manager is also responsible for the second part of the advertising task, that of promoting to the public the media under his control. This frequently involves close co-operation with advertising agencies, since media owners make extensive use of them. However, in some organisations he will also have at his disposal advertising and promotion specialists (as well as executive assistants). This is because the task of promoting a medium to the public calls for continuous liaison with editorial staff so that, at the drop of a hat, the Advertisement Manager is in a position to devise and launch a campaign which exploits a new editorial feature, or a special programme series; to do this frequently necessitates on-the-spot facilities as well as those provided by an agency. Moreover, particularly where women's magazines are concerned, there is a constant need to consider promotion devices: special supplements (cookery, knitting and mothercare, etc.), goods at reduced prices for readers, by arrangement with manufacturers, and free gifts inserted between the covers, all of which are used to sustain interest in a publication and to get new readers.

Although media owners are now as marketing-oriented as the other elements of the advertising industry, the title of Marketing Manager is not yet in wide use. However, his function, that of planning and co-ordinating the total operation, is effectively discharged by the Advertisement Manager. In terms of the personnel under his control the media organisation has close similarity to an advertising agency.

Because of inter-media competition for the advertising £, most media groups have set up central bodies to sell not an individual medium but the *medium-type*. Thus, the British Bureau of Television Advertising (B.B.T.A.), sponsored and financed by the Commercial Television Contractors collectively, promotes the use of television advertising in general. Similar organisations have been established on behalf of provincial evening newspapers, women's magazines, poster advertising and direct mail (i.e., advertising by post).

4. *Ancillary Services*

The advertising industry resembles the car industry in that it makes wide use of a multiplicity of 'component' producers. There are too many of them to be discussed in detail, but further information can be obtained from Advertisers Annual (Business Publications Ltd.). A general list is appended:

Market Research Companies[1]
Advertising Research Companies
Marketing Consultancies
Creative Consultancies
Packaging and Display Consultancies
Exhibition Consultancies (Design and Construction)
Art Studio Services
Photographic Services[1]
Advertisement Printing and Production
Outdoor Advertising Agencies
Public Relations Companies[1]
Premium Supply Houses

[1] These services have professional organisations.

MAIN PROFESSIONAL BODIES CONCERNED WITH ADVERTISING AND MARKETING

ADVERTISING ASSOCIATION, ABFORD HOUSE, 15 WILTON ROAD, LONDON, S.W.1.

This is the collective voice of the advertising industry. All individual bodies of standing are affiliated to the A.A., whose task is to defend and advance the cause of advertising and to ensure that the public interest is served by maintenance of high advertising standards.

The A.A. maintains liaison with Government Departments, industry, education authorities, universities, colleges, schools, consumer associations and other institutions both to put the case for advertising and to keep its finger on the pulse of daily life, in order that advertising remains in step with social as well as commercial development.

The A.A. has a *careers advisory service,* operated on behalf of the industry, to which those seeking a career in advertising should apply for information and advice. Individual membership (as distinct from corporate membership) of the A.A. is not available since its examinations have now been handed to C.A.M. (see Chapter 12).

INSTITUTE OF PRACTITIONERS IN ADVERTISING, 44 BELGRAVE SQUARE, LONDON, S.W.1.

This is the professional body to which leading British advertising agencies, large and small, belong. While its primary task is to represent agency interests, which it does with universally acknowledged efficiency and professionalism, it is also responsible for ensuring that agencies maintain high ethical standards in their dealings with clients, media organisations, suppliers generally and, of course, with each other. The I.P.A. is affiliated to the A.A. and plays an active part in industry affairs.

Individual membership is available only to personnel of *member* agencies, who qualify either by passing the C.A.M. Diploma (see Chapter 12) or by having attained a certain standard of professional experience and status.

INCORPORATED SOCIETY OF BRITISH ADVERTISERS, 45 HERTFORD STREET, LONDON, W.1.

This body represents the interests of advertisers, and its membership includes many companies both large and small. It is an important instrument by which advertisers' collective requirements over a wide range of activities are transmitted to and negotiated with the I.P.A., media organizations and other bodies. I.S.B.A. is affiliated to the A.A. and contributes extensively to industry affairs and to the cause of advertising generally. It maintains close links with all other bodies in advertising, and also with industry and commerce as a whole.

OTHER BODIES

INSTITUTE OF MARKETING, MOOR HALL, COOKHAM, BERKS.

MARKET RESEARCH SOCIETY, 39 HERTFORD STREET, LONDON, W.1.

INSTITUTE OF PUBLIC RELATIONS, TEMPLAR HOUSE, 81–87 HIGH HOLBORN, LONDON, W.C.1.

FOR FURTHER READING

Advertisers' Annual (Business Publications).
Why You Need an Advertising Agency (I.P.A. booklet).
You and the I.P.A. (I.P.A. booklet).

CHAPTER FIVE

Planning an Advertising Campaign

CAMPAIGN PLANNING DEFINED

In novels, films and TV plays, advertising is commonly depicted as a matter of dreaming up slogans and jingles, usually in connection with a miracle product. The task is carried out by people who sit with their feet on the desk seeking inspiration. The reality, of course, is quite different. Just as marketing is more than a matter of making and selling, so advertising is more than slogans and pictures. And the miracle product which completely transcends all others is a rarity, given a universally high standard of technology.

In real life the planning of an advertising campaign is a systematic and carefully organised operation. Inspiration plays a big part in evolving the actual advertising message, but it must be inspiration which is disciplined and relevant. The cleverest words and pictures will make no impression if they say the wrong thing or are directed to the wrong people or appear at the wrong time. At the same time, it is not enough to evolve an advertising proposition which is sound but which lacks sparkle or memorability. There is an old saying in advertising 'get it right and bright' and this is a prime requirement. It calls for the harmonising of technical skills allied to creative flair, and this should be sought in every campaign planning exercise.

Getting it *right* means that the campaign must be related to and be part of the total marketing plan. For example, if the latter calls for an attack on housewives in the 25–44 age group with a new washing powder, then the advertising campaign should be directed at this audience not only in terms of the media used but also in the deployment of selling arguments best calculated to induce this particular audience to purchase. This sounds elementary, but it is surprising how many advertising campaigns, even today, are planned without adequate reference to the total operation; it should be remembered at all times that where there is any element of divorce, mistakes in advertising *direction, content* or *timing* can arise. Therefore, campaign planning is defined as:

> The strategic planning of an advertising and sales promotion campaign which expresses the requirements of marketing strategy.

Getting it *bright* is an integral part of this process, since the greater the understanding among advertising personnel of *each* element of the *total* proposition, the greater the opportunity there is of devising an advertising message which strikes a responsive chord (bearing in mind that consumer benefits may arise in all areas of activity apart from the product itself, e.g., packaging, availability, timing, etc.).

THE CAMPAIGN PLANNING TEAM

The person organising the operation is the agency Account Executive (or Advertising Manager if it is being devised in an advertiser's or media organisation). His job is to obtain the brief from client's marketing or advertising personnel and to transmit it to the agency team who will plan the campaign. He must co-ordinate its activities and, at the final stage, produce a written report which embodies a summary of the advertising proposals, together with a rationale covering each element of the plan. The basic campaign planning team will comprise:

Account Executive,

Creative Team

(The copywriter/scriptwriter and visualiser. These are the personnel who devise the advertising message which appears in newspapers, television, posters, etc.)

Media Planner

(His function is to decide on the means of *delivering* the advertising message, i.e., which medium or media should be employed.)

However, other agency personnel will be called in, as and when required. In a bigger agency, for example, a *Marketing Executive* may be assigned or made available to the team. His task will be to clarify and amplify client's marketing policy and to guide the team in ensuring that advertising policy expresses its requirements. (Many agencies, however, expect their account executives to fulfil this function.)

A *Research Executive* may also be co-opted to interpret available research data and to advise on and obtain further data if necessary, including testing of the advertisements (see Chapter 10). A *Production Executive* may be co-opted to advise on whether a suggested advertisement design or illustration is capable of reproduction in a newspaper or magazine. An agency *Television Producer* will perform a similar role regarding the technicalities involved in translating an advertisement on to the television screen. Most agencies employ such specialists direct; if not they will have access to them on a consultancy or freelance basis, the purpose being to ensure that the campaign is soundly evolved in creative and media terms and that it can be implemented so that advertisements appear to the best advantage and to the time-schedule allocated.

It should, of course, be remembered that all plans have to be submitted to clients and agreed by them. Thus the Account Executive is responsible for *presenting* the agency's proposals to client personnel. Sometimes he will do this solo but it is becoming increasingly common for each member of the agency team to present the *element* of the plan for which he and his subordinates have been responsible. In such cases, it is the Account Executive's responsibility to act as general linkman and, of course, to ensure that all elements form a cohesive and coherent picture when presented.

STEPS IN CAMPAIGN PLANNING

It is important to pursue a logical and soundly disciplined sequence in planning an advertising campaign (or, for that matter, even an individual advertisement). This is because it is essentially a problem-solving operation, and it follows that no one can start to produce a solution until the problem is identified and understood. To put it another way, an advertising campaign is a journey. Until the destination is decided upon, the route cannot be planned.

The following is the correct sequence and, if it is observed in each case, not only are the positive elements of the proposition more easily formulated, but *deficiencies* are more easily exposed. For example, the starting point in campaign planning is *evaluation of the product* in relation to competing products. Provided this is done competently and objectively, its strengths and weaknesses are revealed from the outset. If the latter are likely to be crucial, it is the agency's responsibility to notify the client so that deficiencies can be rectified. It should be remembered that in this way not only is the agency team approaching its own task professionally, it is also acting as a 'long-stop' for client personnel. Thus, it is essential for agency personnel to be marketing oriented, in order that they can both understand the brief they are given and be ready and able to challenge it, in part or whole, if necessary. Most companies welcome the 'safety net' that good agency personnel provide and indeed they expect it to be applied. Just as you do not expect your doctor to tell you what you want to hear, the client does not expect the agency to accept blindly the marketing plan without question.

Under the guidance of the Account Executive, therefore, the campaign planning team will devise its plan on the following basis:

1. *Product Evaluation*

The product to be advertised must be evaluated from all angles: its composition or formula, shape, presentation, colouring, characteristics, performance, packaging and price. Each of these elements must be compared *item for item* with competitive products to establish what advantages it has over them and whether these are meaningful and important to the potential user.

2. *Market Evaluation*

The product must then be analysed in relation to its relevant market-category: the value of this market, market trends, market characteristics (e.g., seasonality) and the competitive situation. Note that current market data is not sufficient. A cumulative picture over at least three years is essential. The data derived from analyses 1 and 2 will determine *the product proposition* (*what* is being sold and *where*).

The next step is to check on the company's capacity to sell it.

3. *Evaluate Company Resources*

The team must check on the size of the company, its financial resources, its scale of operations, its productive capacity, its sales force strength (i.e., its ability to optimise distribution of the product), its product range and all relevant data.

This analysis sets the PARAMETERS of marketing and advertising activity.

Thus having established the proposition, the market in which it is to be sold and the general scale of operations, the next step is to measure them against the company's marketing objectives (or, if these have not been finalised by this stage, to establish them in conjunction with client personnel).

4. *Marketing Objectives*

These represent *what* is to be achieved with the *total* proposition in relation to available resources. By correlating objectives and resources, any lack of realism is immediately exposed. (E.g., if resources are limited it is useless in most cases to strive for major market shares.)

Marketing objectives, like all objectives, should be precise and capable of measurement, e.g.:

To increase distribution of Product A in independent chemists from 75% (present level) to 90% in the next 12 months. To increase market share of Product B nationally from 12% to 14%.

Note that marketing objectives embrace other factors apart from actual sales. Sales forecasts should, however, be included in the list of objectives.

The next step is to check or devise the marketing strategy which, in the judgement of those involved, is most capable of fulfilling the objectives.

5. *Marketing Strategy*

This is the total plan which establishes the *marketing mix* to be employed and the degree of emphasis to be placed on each element within it.

6. *The Marketing Budget*

Now that the total plan and the role of each element within it has been agreed or confirmed, the overall budget can now be established. This is fixed as a total sum (usually on the basis of the task in relation to sales requirements) which is then broken down and allocated to each element of the chosen marketing mix, in line with the emphases already selected. Thus, the money made available for advertising will reflect the importance of its part in the operation both in terms of objectives and task.

7. *Sales Plan*

The company's sales force will play a vital part in the total operation in terms of sustaining and extending distribution of the product, motivating the retailer not only to stock it but also to display (i.e., expose) it prominently and, of course, in maximising sales into the shops. The agency team will want details of the sales operation and indeed may well contribute ideas, particularly in terms of devising incentives for the trade and for the sales force itself. The timing of the advertising campaign must also be carefully co-ordinated with the sales operation; i.e., the product must be in the shops *prior* to the commencement of advertising to the public, with supporting product display material which reflects the theme of the new advertising.

At this point, it will be seen that the agency team has confirmed or even established the necessary marketing framework in which to plan the actual advertising campaign itself: the proposition, the market to be tackled, realistic marketing objectives, marketing strategy (the total plan), the money allocated for all purposes, including advertising, and the sales plan with which to ensure that the product will be available and exposed to the consumer at point of sale.

Just as the *groundwork* for campaign planning is a disciplined and systematic operation, so is the *planning itself*. Thus, the starting point is to *pre-determine* what the campaign is to achieve.

8. *Establish Advertising Objectives*

These should not be confused with marketing objectives. Neither should they be related specifically to sales because, although the influence of advertising on sales is in most cases considerable, it is extremely difficult to isolate the *precise* degree of influence[1] (see Chapter 6). Therefore advertising objectives should be expressed in terms of COMMUNICATION. Nevertheless, wherever possible they should be precise and capable of measurement, e.g.:

To increase awareness of Brand A among housewives 25–44, the increase to be from the present 30% to 40% after 12 months.

To obtain an average of 12 'leads' (i.e., enquiries) per week per salesman for industrial product B.

9. *Advertising Strategy*

Having decided advertising objectives, the next step is to decide *what* is going to be done to achieve them. This is when the basic decisions are taken in regard to the *duration* of the campaign, the target audience, the elements of the proposition to be promoted, in short the total plan of approach.

The *implementation* of this strategy is in two parts and will be undertaken specifically by the appropriate specialists.

Creative Planning = *creating* the advertising message
Media Planning = *delivering* the advertising message

(See Chapter 7 and 8 for more detailed summaries of the key aspects of these operations.)

10. *Creative Planning*

This sub-divides into three parts:

(A) *Objectives*. These should not be confused with the *total* advertising objectives (which are achieved by the *message* and the *delivery* in combination) but should relate to the communication factors which the campaign is to project.

(B) *Strategy*. This is the *platform* on which they will be projected (e.g., exploitation of the product's speed of action because of special ingredients).

[1] Except in mail order, where advertising is the dominant element of the marketing mix.

(C) *Execution.* This is the physical expression of the campaign in terms of the written words and advertising design and presentation. (For pre- and post-testing of advertisements see Chapter 10.)

11. *Media Planning*

This sub-divides into two parts:

(A) *Objectives.* Here the media planner has to establish what the plan must achieve, within the available budget, in terms of economical *coverage* of the target audience and the *frequency* of exposure.

(B) *Plan.* This embodies the basis of *actual* media selection in relation to the budget and of creative requirements, i.e. details of target audience coverage and exposure frequency, together with a *schedule* which indicates the viewership or readership of each medium selected and the times or dates when the advertisements will appear.

12. *Sales Promotion*

Where sales promotion (or 'below the line' activity) is called for, it should, of course, be regarded as an integral part of advertising strategy and not as an 'extra'.

The same criteria of approach should be adopted in this area as in all other areas.

(i) *Establish objectives.* This is important since it is essential to pre-determine what sales promotion activity is to achieve, e.g., to induce consumer trial purchasing, to stimulate extended consumption by existing users. (See Chapter 9)

(ii) *Establish strategy.* The foregoing will play a large part in determining the selection of the sales promotion approach or approaches to be adopted, the range of which is discussed in Chapter 9.

FOR FURTHER READING

Campaign Planning (Olaf Ellefsen, Business Books Ltd. for I.P.A.).
Advertising in Action (Harris and Selden, Hutchinson Publishing Group Ltd.).
Case Studies in Marketing (G. B. Giles, Macdonald & Evans Ltd.).
Lane's Advertising Administration (N. T. Sandbrook, and L. Livesey, Butterworth & Co. Ltd.).

Note

The last chapter discussed the procedures involved in campaign planning which comprise the establishment of a marketing framework, together with the sequence of events in relation to specific advertising operations. The latter involves the solution of four basic problems:

(i) deciding the advertising appropriation
(ii) creating the advertising message
(iii) delivering the advertising message
(iv) planning and devising sales promotion activity.

The next four chapters take a closer look at these problems.

CHAPTER SIX

Deciding the Advertising Appropriation

FACTORS WHICH INFLUENCE SALES

ADVERTISING, of course, influences sales. The problem is to determine the degree to which it does so. This is of more than academic interest to the individual company when faced with the task of deciding, for a given project, what to spend on advertising.

The first thing to understand is that it is a difficult and complex undertaking to isolate one selling influence from all the selling influences which are brought to bear in each situation. We have already seen that these comprise a wide range of activities known as the marketing mix. But these are *internal* influences, that is they are under the manufacturer's control. His sales, however, may also be affected by *external* influences, over which he has no direct control (although, of course, he can take action by way of anticipation or response to those influences). These are many in number but to make the point it is necessary only to take three examples:

THE ECONOMY

In a buoyant economy consumer demand is high, but during a credit squeeze consumer purchasing power is reduced and thus demand falls off. This can affect many markets and products as well as the more obvious high-priced durables. For example, retailers in all fields tend to reduce their stock inventories in order to minimise bank-borrowing and thus interest repayments. Not only can this lead to a reduction in the manufacturer's factory sales, it can also reduce consumer purchasing since lower stocks may well lead to a lower level of brand exposure at retail, with a resultant drop in consumer awareness and of impulse purchasing.

COMPETITION

An increase in activity by one manufacturer can, in an expanding market, increase sales of his competitors' brands as well as his own. However, in a static or declining market, his sales may be gained at their expense, although in either case their efforts may remain the same.

THE WEATHER

A hot summer can create greater demand for beer, soft drinks, ice cream, sun glasses, etc. A bad winter can do the same for soups, cough remedies, overcoats, etc. Thus in one year a manufacturer's sales can be £X while in the next, due to favourable conditions over which he has no control, sales are £X + £Y, although his marketing expenditure may not have altered.

All this underlines the difficulties involved in isolating the effectiveness of advertising, bearing in mind that the variables referred to can differ from market to market and indeed from project to project. Therefore, in most cases it is impossible to determine the precise effect on sales of given levels of advertising expenditure. It follows then that there is no set formula for deciding an advertising appropriation. However, there are a number of *procedures,* which we will now examine.

MOST COMMON METHODS OF DECIDING THE ADVERTISING APPROPRIATION

Since advertising expenditure is a marketing cost it must be related to revenue (as indeed must every other activity). However, although revenue is the ultimate *discipline,* to use it as the sole *determinant* of appropriation setting is not the ideal approach, as the following common methods indicate. (Note the distinction between 'discipline' and 'determinant'.)

1. *Fixed Percentage of Past Sales to Determine Advertising Appropriation for Future Sales* (Historic method)

Advantage: Money already earned thus the advertising appropriation can be afforded.

Disadvantage: When sales are good, more money is spent on advertising. When they are bad, less is spent. It is obvious that this may well be wrong because, if sales do take a downward trend, this trend can be perpetuated by such a policy.

2. *Fixed percentage of Future Sales*

Advantage: A good discipline, one which encourages more accurate sales forecasting.

Disadvantage: The same as for the historic method, namely more advertising expenditure when sales are likely to be good, less when they are likely to be bad, again with an in-built tendency to drive a slump further downwards.

3. *Spending at the Same Rate as Competition*

Advantage: Can help to avoid an 'advertising war'.

Disadvantage: Parity is only possible in terms of media advertising since it is almost impossible to measure below the line activity with great accuracy.

This method also fails to take account of other variables (e.g., competitors may be more active in terms of other elements of their marketing mix or they may have different objectives).

4. *Whatever can be Afforded*

Advantage: It sets a limit on what is spent.

Disadvantage: This can lead to underspending or overspending since it is not related to the advertising task.

5. *Advertising/Profit joint residuum*

This method is based on calculating *gross* profits from a targeted level of sales, from which a figure for advertising is deducted in order to arrive at a *net* profit.

Example:

Brand A:	Projected Sales Revenue	£200,000
	Deduct cost of goods and other overheads	£130,000
	Available for profit/advertising	£70,000

Advantage: Shows profit-orientation, a quality which is indispensable to the modern advertising professional.

Disadvantage: The temptation here is to take too much for profit, leaving too little for advertising. Even more importantly, however, an advertising appropriation should never be allocated arbitrarily but in relation to set objectives and thus the task which has to be carried out (see Chapter 5).

It will be seen therefore that none of the foregoing methods are satisfactory in themselves in that they do not meet the objective-task criterion. Methods 1 and 2, singly or in combination, are probably employed by the majority of advertisers, although they are increasingly being regarded as *discipline reference points* rather than as the sole means of deciding the appropriation.

Thus when the appropriation is set as a percentage either of past or future sales (bearing in mind that past experience of a given brand may indicate such a correlation between advertising and sales) some advertisers will then consider whether any *weighting factors* should be applied. This simply means that what is essentially an accountancy calculation is subjected to re-scrutiny in the light of current marketing conditions. Rather than attempt a wordy explanation it is perhaps better to demonstrate it.

One example of weighting

Present situation

Brand A:	Brand leader in packaged drug field.
Share of Market:	18%
Past advertising to sales ratio:	25%
Usual method of fixing appropriation:	25% of future sales.
Present position:	Sales levelling out. Analysis of market situation suggests that more advertising support needed to maintain product franchise in the light of increased competition.

Conclusion: Present advertising to sales ratio inadequate' since it is geared to brand sales only and not to new factors which have arisen in the market.

Implication: Company must be prepared, *if necessary,* to accept lower immediate profit return by raising its advertising to help protect its long-term position in this market.

Weighting method used:

Brand A's share of market: 18%

Brand A's share of total advertising in this market: 16% (at prevailing advertising to sales ratio)

For major brands, their *share* of total advertising must be at least equal to their share of market (in some markets it should be greater). In this case Brand A's advertising is not and in the longer-term interests of the brand it ought to be. Thus Brand A's advertising appropriation at rate equal to par equals the final appropriation, viz:

Brand A's advertising appropriation based on sales estimate only = £X.

Additional expenditure to increase Brand A's share of total advertising to equal its share of market (weighting factor) = £XY.

This example is given to provide one practical demonstration of how a weighting might be applied, although it is emphasised that the degree of weighting and the technique used depend upon the individual problem.

However, the ideal way to approach the appropriation-setting problem is to return to fundamental principles (without which it will be difficult, in any case, even to apply disciplined weightings to common appropriation-fixing methods). These turn on the basic issues outlined in Chapter 5, namely the establishment of *objectives* (where you want to be) and *task* (what you need to get there). In Walter Taplin's book 'Advertising Appropriation Policy' the following are listed as the key factors in setting the advertising appropriation:

1. Assembling and evaluation of all relevant data.
2. A comprehensive marketing Plan.
3. A task-setting budget.
4. Constant Check on performance.
5. Maximum flexibility throughout the budget period.

All students are advised to read this excellent book; although it is out of print, most libraries have copies of it.

FOR FURTHER READING

Advertising Appropriation Policy (Walter Taplin, I.P.A. booklet).
How to Budget for Industrial Advertising (I.P.A. booklet).
Costing for Advertising (R. Brandon, Bailey Brothers).

CHAPTER SEVEN

Creating the Advertising Message

UNDERSTANDING PEOPLE

ADVERTISING is advocacy. It is concerned with motivating people. However, before you can motivate people you have to understand them. Thus a proper understanding of people is essential to the advertising man and woman, as indeed it is to politicians, entertainers, salesmen, personnel managers and all whose task it is to influence other human beings.

To talk about understanding people is easy enough. To achieve it is quite another matter. As any personnel manager knows, human beings embody a wide range of needs and impulses, sometimes exasperatingly so. In their work, these needs and impulses cannot be satisfied by money alone, important though it is. People seek other things besides salaries and wages. They want individual identity. They want the importance of the job they do, and thus of themselves, to be fully recognised. They want status and commensurate privileges which demonstrate possession of it. They set great store by the human face of their working conditions, in terms of how accessible management is, how reasonable it is in its dealings with employees, how enlightened it is in consultation and communication, how fair the system of promotion is and, not least, how friendly their colleagues are. A job, therefore, is more than something which provides the employee's bread and butter. It is an integral part of life and, under the right conditions, it should be a source of wide-ranging satisfactions.

Note the word *satisfactions*. People seek satisfactions not things. This concept is particularly important in marketing and advertising; it is based on the recognition that people do not buy products, they buy satisfactions. Take face powder as an example. Any chemist can make it. It is not difficult to formulate nor to mix. The result could be plainly packaged and offered for sale fairly cheaply. As a number of retail chemists have discovered, few women are interested. To provide satisfaction, face powder has to be attractively packaged and presented. It has to have an inviting scent. It has to carry an aura of glamour. In short, the woman seeks not a box of powder as such but the promise of beauty—and the promise is absent when the proposition is boiled down to something of mere utility. The same principle operates in everything we buy. A car is not a piece of machinery nor even solely a means of transport. It is a satisfaction wherein we express our desire for freedom to go wherever we please and to demonstrate to others our capacity to do so.

Quite clearly, therefore, if we are in the advertising business we have to reach a *disciplined* understanding of human motivation. In our everyday lives as individuals we might get by with the kind of pragmatic understanding of people that is restricted to those we deal with, our relatives, friends, colleagues, etc. In advertising we require a more systematic and broadly based knowledge of motivation.

It is possible only to touch upon human motivation in this book and students should certainly go into this all-important subject much more deeply (see reading list at the end of this Chapter). In broad outline, however, it turns upon *drives towards the satisfaction of needs.* There are two kinds of human needs: primary and secondary.

Primary needs divide into four: shelter, security, sustenance and sex. In other words, we must have somewhere to live and to sleep; we must have the security of human affection, hence the family unit (and beyond this the community for mutual self-protection); we must have food in order to live; we need sex not only to have children but also as a fundamental means of physical and emotional expression. Little needs to be said about these human requirements. They add up to the desire for life, the instinct for self-survival. Where advertising is concerned, it touches them endemically rather than specifically. Recognition of their existence is at its core and must be omnipresent. (E.g., main foods in advertising *must always be associated with nourishment*—which is basic—as well as with taste and appearance.)

Secondary needs can be summed up as being social needs in contra-distinction to basic needs. (The satisfaction of social needs is important; the satisfaction of basic needs is vital.) Social needs tend not to vary in principle between one form of society and another. Whether we look at Ancient Rome or Modern Britain we see the same social drives: the desire for social status, individual recognition, material advancement. What is different today, of course, is the *expression* given to these social needs now that we live in a mass-consumption democracy. In advertising they have to be recognised not only *in toto* but also in relation to specific propositions, bearing in mind that social needs cover a broad spectrum and that they can vary from one human activity to another.

How can we translate the foregoing principles into concrete examples of human motivation? By analysing and then breaking down the main characteristics of behaviour we can start to build up a better *formal* understanding of the drives involved. These, in fact, divide into four categories:

All of us want to *be* something = attainment
All of us want to *achieve* something = ambition
All of us want to *do* something = action
All of us want to *avoid* something = prevention.

Attainment (examples of)

We want to be healthy; attractive; successful (e.g., in our jobs, as parents, etc.); capable; influential over others; admired by others; possess self-confidence.

Ambition (examples of)

We want to retain our health; better appearance; more money; more security; popularity; increased prestige; greater convenience and comfort; pride of accomplishment; more leisure.

Action (examples of)

We want to express ourselves (e.g., at work, at leisure, etc); acquire possessions; copy those we admire; take action to improve our social status.

Prevention (examples of)

We want to avoid effort; anxiety; uncertainty; embarrassment; wasting time; spending money on things which do not satisfy us.

These elements may then be crystallised into priorities, i.e., the most important of these drives, viz:

Improved health
More money
Security
Better appearance
Social advancement
Success
Greater popularity
Esteem of others
More comfort and convenience
Increased enjoyment and leisure
Pride of accomplishment.

In advertising it is the Creative team's task, and that of the copywriter in particular, to identify those needs which are relevant to the consumer *and* which can be satisfied by the product or service being advertised, and then to express the benefits of the proposition in a way which is convincing and memorable.

CREATING THE ADVERTISING MESSAGE: BASIC PRINCIPLES

Must express Marketing Strategy

The first principle is that advertising must express the requirements of marketing strategy. In Chapter 5, we traced the steps taken in campaign planning, wherein the creative team are exposed to and indeed involved in the development of the total plan. If the plan is consumer-oriented, it should embody a *total* proposition which meets the needs and desires of the target-audience. It is then the task of the creative team to *isolate* and to express in the advertising *those elements of the proposition* which are most likely to motivate the consumer to purchase.

Choosing Primary and Secondary Appeals

An advertising campaign is rather like a shop window. The retailer has a range of goods for sale inside the shop. To get people inside he has to feature in his window the goods which have the greatest appeal. To put unsuitable goods in his window creates a barrier. To put too many goods in achieves the kind of clutter in which it is impossible to determine what the retailer is selling. (We have all seen such shop windows where emphasis on everything is emphasis on nothing.) Advertising must observe the same principle. It must expose the right appeal, and it must not fall into the trap of overloading the 'window'. And, like the shop window, advertising has certain limitations. It cannot by itself clinch the sale, but it can act as a potent contributory factor by creating awareness and the right attitude towards the product.

Choosing the right *primary appeal* is of fundamental importance in advertising. If an error is made here the campaign is likely to be largely wasted, no matter how right everything else may be. This is why it is vital for the creative team no less than anyone else to study whatever market research data is available. It is essential to establish as much information as possible about consumer needs and wants in relation to the product, remembering at the same time that the majority principle must be observed. In other words, the appeal which is evolved must be based on the needs and wants of the greatest number of people within the target audience. This is the major difference between face-to-face selling and advertising.

An Anadin advertisement from a press campaign which ran for almost ten years without major change. Anadin's special formula supports a broadly based claim; in this case it centres on the promise of relief from tense nervous headaches, which are a common feature of modern life. Thus the advertisement has wide appeal yet remains specific, authoritative and cogent. Note the highly individual visual approach—no possibility here of Anadin being confused with any other headache remedy

(Reproduced by courtesy of International Chemical Company Ltd.)

The former can be adapted to the individual; thus the salesman is concerned with how *different* people are, in order to achieve the maximum degree of motivation with each potential customer. Advertising is directed to large groups of people; therefore, it is important to establish how much *alike* they are in order to find common motivational denominators.

It would, of course, be misleading to suggest that research data provides all the answers. It provides facts; such facts will only rarely be available in sufficient range and depth as to vitiate the need for skilled judgements. Let us take an example from real life. Some years ago a company marketing a new method of learning shorthand, which takes weeks instead of months to learn, was faced with the problem of isolating the most potent advertising appeal from a range of possibilities. Girls want to learn shorthand in order to earn more money. They also want the prestige of being a secretary and of gaining the opportunity of meeting interesting people. However, learning shorthand can be a tedious and lengthy business and this acts as a tremendous barrier to many would-be learners. The research data (necessarily limited because of the limited resources of the company) showed that all these factors were important motivationally. *On which appeal did the company major?* It went straight to the core of the problem by spearheading the speed and simplicity of its method of teaching. Most girls knew already they could earn more money and greater prestige by writing shorthand. What they did not know was that a new method existed which cut out much of the tedium and drudgery of learning it. This was the *real* proposition. The method itself could not deliver the end-benefits, but it could overcome an obstacle to their attainment.

Selecting the right supporting arguments, or what is known as

---

This still from a Homepride TV commercial is part of a campaign which has promoted the product benefits memorably and convincingly. The charm and humour of Fred and his fellow flour-graders has created a unique personality for the brand and tremendous goodwill among the public
(Reproduced by courtesy of Spillers Ltd. Agency: Geers Gross Advertising Ltd.)

secondary appeals is also important. In the shorthand case there was clearly a need to provide re-assurance about the method. Discussions with would-be secretaries revealed there were two main question marks in regard to it. Was the system acceptable to employers? (pointless to spend time and money on learning something which might not be usable). Was it *really* that easy to learn? The key secondary appeals, therefore, were based upon *evidence* that employers welcomed girls who had learned this method (a list of important companies was given who employed such girls) and the offer of a free trial lesson, which said *prove* for yourself that the method is simple and easy to learn.

This company's advertising was successful because it said the right things and it said them in the right order. It answered consumer needs in a way which was entirely relevant. Yet other advertisers could have cluttered up the proposition with hyperbole about salaries and prestige and, by so doing, diverted attention from what was really being sold: a new method of shorthand.

Selling Benefits

It is an axiom that salesmen must sell benefits. That is they must present the proposition not from the standpoint of the seller but in terms of how and why it can benefit the buyer. Since advertising is selling too, this is a principle which must be observed at all times. It can be over-looked.

The reason is not hard to find. Manufacturers and sponsors of services are closely involved in what they produce. Because of this they are aware of all sorts of qualities their goods and services possess. These qualities may be admired and respected not only in the company itself but also by the industry at large. Frequently they represent considerable technical or administrative achievement. Not unnaturally, there is the temptation to tell the customer all about them in the advertising. However, unless they can be translated into relevant and important consumer benefits, the advertising will misfire badly. People are seldom interested in a product or service in itself. Their interest lies in *what it can do for them.*

Take insurance. The prospect is not interested in how long the company has been established, what its total assets are and that its watchword is security and has been since seventeen hundred and something. (Factors which are no doubt a tremendous source of pride to its management.) What he wants to know is what he will have to pay to be insured for certain sums of money, what bonuses, if any, will accrue to him and what tax relief is available. The advertising may well re-inforce consumer benefits with some reassurance about the standing of the company, but this is usually only of marginal value. The major element must always be the promotion of benefits to the potential buyer. These must nearly always embody relevant *information*. There is nothing more irritating to the consumer than to be exposed to an advertisement—say—for a refrigerator which omits to mention its capacity or its price. Remember that one of the principal benefits of advertising is the provision of information, information relevant to the prospect's needs and wants.

Keeping the Promise

As you will see from Chapter 11, there are formidable regulations in advertising to curb exaggerated, misleading or false claims. Even if these did not exist, such practice is undesirable. Check this statement against your own experience of life. If someone makes a promise to you and breaks it, you lose confidence in that person. An advertisement is a promise: moreover it is one made publicly, in the open market place. If the sponsor of it wants to remain in business he has to ensure that his promises are kept at all times. The consumer will make some allowance for hyperbole, or what is called 'puffery'. Enthusiasm in advertising is expected and indeed necessary. What is commercially (and morally) wrong are claims about a product or service which it cannot live up to. A disappointed consumer seldom, if ever, re-purchases a product over which he or she has been misled. And it scarcely needs saying that repeat business is the life-blood of any company.

The creative team has a special responsibility to check product performance against the claims it wishes to make. If it falls short of them it is imperative to amend or withdraw these claims, or for the manufacturer to bring the product up to the standard indicated. Creative

Here are six successful advertisements, successful that is in terms of their capacity to project an advertising proposition succinctly, persuasively and memorably. All are outdoor, a very difficult medium in which to devise the advertising message because of the need for instant communication.

These advertisements are a selection from those which won awards in the 1970 Poster Design Awards sponsored by the Council for Industrial Design.

Advertiser: Way In
Agency: Papart, Koening Lois Ltd.
Designer: Paul Walter
Printer: St. Michael's Press Ltd.
C.I.D. Judges' Comment: Select their target audience carefully; delicately done

(Reproduced by courtesy of Council for Industrial Design)

Advertiser: British Rail Western Region
Agency: Ogilvy and Mather Ltd.
Designer: Peter Rivers
Printer: The Century Litho Platemaking Company
C.I.D. Judges' Comment: The best visual idea among the posters submitted, tellings its story quickly, completely and with wit

(Reproduced by courstey of Council for Industrial Design)

Advertiser: London Transport
Agency: S. H. Benson Ltd.
Designer: Malcolm McDonald
(*Copy:* Phillip Thomas)
Printer: Hampden Press Ltd.
C.I.D. Judges' Comment: A campaign aimed at media men and as such a good way to advertise a particularly challenging site; good copy clearly laid out

(Reproduced by courtesy of Council for Industrial Design)

Advertiser: Health Education Council
Creative Consultants: Cramer Saatchi Ltd.
Designer: John Hegarty
(*Copy:* Michael Coughlan)
Printer: Protyprint Ltd.
C.I.D. Judges' Comment: Strong copy putting its message across effectively

(Reproduced by courtesy of Council for Industrial Design)

Male or female, you're all the same to us at the Way In.

Our latest range of clothes looks just as good on the weaker sex as it does on the strong one.

Come in and try a few things on.

We've got one-sex trousers, shirts, coats, hats, and swimwear. All in two-sex sizes.

One warning. If you come in to buy a surprise present for your nearest and dearest, be careful.

They might be there buying one for you.

Open Tuesday through Friday till 7pm.
Saturdays till 5pm. Closed Monday.
Way In, Hans Crescent, Knightsbridge, S.W.1.

One-sex clothes in two-sex sizes.

Horizontal Hotels Limited, Western Group.

Ordinary Stock: smooth, fast Inter-City Sleepers. Central heating. Fitted carpets. Wash basins, H & C running water. Fresh towels and soap. Shaver points. Fingertip lighting controls. Moving view from windows. Principal assets: soft white bed with crisp white sheets. Liquid assets: coffee or tea in bed next morning (or any time). Extraordinary Stock: Motorail Sleepers to take over your car as well. Dividends: you sleep the night and gain a day. Horizontal hotels glide every night from Inter-City centres in the West to London and the North, and from South Wales to London.

Make Inter-City your permanent way-there and back.

Your shoes won't really need cleaning. They go hundreds of miles on Inter-City without losing their polish. Ask for the free pocket timetable with details of this overnight network. It's a profitable investment. Sleep on it.

This poster is 12 miles long.
London Transport Advertising 836 3456
SF 1
LONDON TRANSPORT

This is what happens when a fly lands on your food.

Flies can't eat solid food, so to soften it up they vomit on it.

Then they stamp the vomit in until it's a liquid, usually stamping in a few germs for good measure.

Then when it's good and runny they suck it all back again, probably dropping some excrement at the same time.

And then, when they've finished eating, it's your turn.

Cover food. Cover eating and drinking utensils. Cover dustbins.

The Health Education Council

And another reason to see
The Gardening Centre.
And a blooming
good reason at that:
12,000 roses. 400
different varieties.
All longing to be sniffed.
(My word, Sir, you've
got just the nose
they're after.)
Rose Season:
June - September.
Hours of entry:
from 10.30 a.m. Open daily
until October 31st.
Admission: Adults 5/-;
old age pensioners/
16 years and under 2/6d.
Free parking.
No dogs (sorry dogs).
Details of party rates and
Season Tickets from the
Administration Department:
The Gardening Centre,
Syon Park, Brentford,
Middlesex. Tel: 01-560 0881
The greatest gardening show on earth.

wakey
wakey!

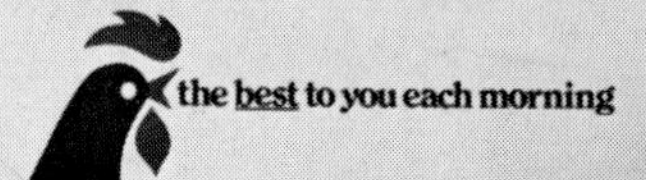

FAIRY
Brillo

IBM

Advertiser: The Gardening Centre Ltd.
Agency: Graham & Gillies Ltd.
Designer: Rex Guildford
Printer: Leigh Print and Display Ltd.
C.I.D. Judges' Comment: Consistent use of graphics throughout the series; both the images and the words are relevant; an effective treatment
(Reproduced by courtesy of Council for Industrial Design)

Advertiser: Kellogg Co. of Great Britain Ltd.
Agency: J. Walter Thompson Ltd.
Designer: Agency group
Printer: Hindson Reid and Jordison Ltd.
C.I.D. Judges' Comment: Intriguing set of posters which both puzzle and involve the viewer; an imaginative presentation for a good product
(Reproduced by courtesy of Council for Industrial Design)

A retail audit in progress. By checking the retailer's stock against the previous audit (and taking into account what new stock has been supplied since that time), the amount the retailer has sold over the period is determined—both totally and brand-by-brand
(Photograph by courtesy of A. C. Nielsen Co. Ltd.)

Computers are widely used in market research operations to process wide-ranging and often complex data. Here is part of an extensive IBM installation at work in the British H.Q. of the world's biggest market research company
(Photograph by courtesy of A. C. Nielsen Co. Ltd.)

people should resist attempts to be pressurised, or to give in to the temptation of making claims which, if untrue, can damage the longer-term interests of the brand as well as help bring all advertising into disrepute.

The Need to Gain Attention

No advertisement ever appears in a vacuum. In a newspaper, for example, it competes for the readers' attention with the news, with editorial features and with other advertisements. On television or cinema-screen, an advertisement is quickly followed by another or by the programme matter. The poster has to get over its message with a lot of other messages (and distractions) to people walking or riding down a busy street and who will pass by very quickly. A direct mail letter competes with business and personal mail. Thus an advertisement must compel attention. If it is unnoticed, or ignored, it has failed.

Some advertisers fall into the trap of equating attention-getting with the use of screaming headlines in newspapers or, on TV, with explosive visual and sound effects. The trouble with this is that if other people are doing this (including the media themselves)—and unfortunately they often are—the impact of such devices can often be lost in a welter of typematter or noise. If everyone shouts, how can the shouting of one person be heard? Moreover, when attention *is* gained in this way, its shock value quickly fades and on further exposure it either irritates the reader or viewer, or bores him or fails to register altogether. The same is true about other attention-getting devices commonly in use. 'Catchpenny' headlines of a sensational nature can attract immediate attention, but if they are irrelevant to the proposition, or they create an expectation which is not satisfied, the reader or viewer quickly loses interest. This is cheating and the consumer knows it.

If these devices are wrong, what are the right ones? There is no set answer to this. Basically the solution turns on achieving *distinctiveness,* that is producing an advertisement which, in a given context, stands out. Distinctiveness can take many forms. It can derive from skilful *advertisement design,* i.e., the disposing of the elements in a way which is unusual yet coherent (it must facilitate further study and understanding as well as to attract attention). It can stem from creative *typography*, e.g., the use of a stylish yet forceful script in a context which is likely to be jam-packed with conventional type-matter. It can hinge on an *illustration* which in content or execution is arresting and intriguing. It can be based on *words* alone, for example a headline which poses a problem or states a proposition of considerable interest to a given group of people. It can be, and often is, achieved by a *combination of* all these elements. At the end of this chapter you will find examples of successful advertisements. Among their other merits, they have the merit of being able to achieve attention (even when they are fighting for it in the real-life situation). They do so by offering the target audience some reward for its time and attention, in terms of news, benefits or novelty. All of them induce the reader to go beyond the headlines and picture. This is what attention is all about: to attract the reader or viewer to an advertisement, to open the door as it were to what is inside.

Sustaining Interest

Having gained the attention of the prospect it is clearly of vital importance to sustain it. Some advertisers seek to solve the problem by postponing for as long as possible the deployment of selling arguments. Most of you must have seen TV commercials which spend a long time in scene-setting or in entertaining, with the 'sell' crammed into the last few seconds. This is a ploy which is fairly common. It derives from a belief that the product being advertised has no intrinsic interest; the only way to hold the prospect, therefore, is to divert attention from it and then, by sleight of hand, to slip in the 'plug' towards the end.

This, of course, is quite wrong. The whole purpose of advertising is to sell products and services and it is on these that the main emphasis should be placed. The creative challenge is to do this in a way which is *interesting to the prospect and yet succeeds in getting across the relevant selling points*. As it happens, the inhibitions which some advertising people have about products are unjustified. The consumer constantly seeks satisfaction; clearly, successful products provide satisfactions and this being so they must possess points of interest which can be exploited in the advertising message. (Where *new* products are concerned, the opportunity for creating and sustaining interest, given the advantage of novelty or of new benefits, scarcely needs stressing.)

This is an important principle. Sustain interest but ensure that it is in terms of the product or service being advertised. In Britain Oxo advertising over the past few years provides a perfect demonstration of how this can be done. Oxo is a flavouring agent and, although it is a good and useful product, it does not appear, at first glance, to provide much scope for interesting advertising. But the 'Katie and Philip' series has created an awareness of and interest in Oxo which has revitalised the brand. It has, of course, tremendous human interest—people are interested in people—and large sections of the public have become as involved in these characters as those who appear in 'Coronation Street', but this is not gained at the expense of the product. The situation is always created wherein the product benefits can be demonstrated. The dishes prepared by Katie show how Oxo can be used to add flavour to a meal—they also, of course, suggest how its uses can be extended.

Given the apparently limited scope of the product, you will readily see how inhibited creative people could have side-stepped the issue of selling it. The agency (J. Walter Thompson) met the problem head on and solved it brilliantly. In so doing it avoided the reverse trap. Just as there are those who evade the product, as it were, there are others who go in for product worship. Typical examples of this are the commericals which catalogue selling points endlessly. This is not the way to sustain interest. Consumers quickly get bored by the 'catalogue' approach and when their interest fades the selling effectiveness of the advertisement fades with it.

Creating Desire . . . Inducing Action

Obviously one of the most important tasks in advertising is to create desire. It sounds simple enough but there are traps for the unwary. To avoid them it is important to bear in mind first principles, namely that people buy satisfactions not goods. The product or service being advertised, therefore, has to be converted by the advertiser into ultimate satisfaction before desire can be aroused. Long ago an American advertising man coined the phrase 'sell the sizzle not the steak' and although this is now an advertising cliché its validity is unshakable. A slab of meat in itself is unlikely to create desire, but to show it cooked and piping hot, surrounded by vegetables, turns an object into a proposition. The Oxo advertising, referred to earlier, observes the same principle. The cube itself does not create desire: it is its relationship to tasty dishes which activates appetite-appeal.

Food advertisers, in fact, understand this principle better than most, although, of course, the creation of desire for food is relatively easy because it involves a fundamental instinct. However, another group of advertisers who are skilled in activating desire are the film production companies. The 'trailer' highlights the most dramatic or amusing elements of the forthcoming film with practised urgency and cogency, and this can be a very potent means among audiences of creating desire to see the film thus advertised.

The key to desire is, of course, involvement, or what psychologists call *empathy*. It is a word which means feeling with active sympathy, e.g., supporters of a football team wince and even perform mental tackles when its goal is under attack. Empathy takes place when the viewer or reader becomes drawn into, and achieves self-identification with, the story or action. Such involvement is more difficult to achieve in advertising because of the shortness of the message and it underlines the need to demonstrate not what a product is but what it *does* (i.e., what satisfaction it can deliver). Toothpaste is not a strip of cream on a brush but a fresh mouth, a tingle, a waking-up. Milk is not a commodity but a source of vitality, energy, refreshment. Paint is not a liquid in a can but the means of transforming a house or room. Selling the sizzle not the steak creates desire—and desire is a major step towards product purchase.

However, there is still one more step: actual purchase. To induce action at this point is not easy, given the range of distractions and pressures to which most people are subjected. Now, as you will have seen from Chapter 2, the modern marketing operation brings other action-influences to bear besides advertising. Product distribution and display is one such (vital) influence. By ensuring that the product is available and exposed in retail outlets, an important link is forged between advertising and point of sale, one which re-inforces the spur to action. Actual buying incentives through sales promotion devices (see Chapter 9) can strengthen it still further.

This is not to suggest that advertising cannot induce action. Of course it can, but the extent of competition today discourages over-reliance on any single element of the marketing mix, including advertising. However, regardless of other elements, every advertisement itself should actively encourage the consumer to take action. This is less a matter of 'buy it today' or 'buy it now' (although such phrases are probably mandatory in many cases) as the degree of urgency which the advertisement generates overall. This urgency should be sustained right through to the sign-off. Where there is an *incentive* to purchase, e.g., a free trial or money-off offer, this should be featured prominently. Even when this is not available it should never be overlooked that among other things *convenience* is an incentive. Most people are lazy. They are reassured if little effort is likely to be involved in their actions. A coupon to fill in is an obvious example of making it easy for the consumer to take action (so much so that there is always a 10% lunatic fringe of 'professional' coupon-fillers). This, of course, does not apply in many cases, but the principle should be observed whenever possible. The promise of 'at your local dealer *now*' or 'from Boots, Woolworths and all stores' is not to be despised since it indicates that action is not difficult to take. You may even be lucky enough one day to be able to sign-off with 'while stocks last' or 'available for a limited period only', which is a near-certain way of getting some action if the proposition is right to begin with!

Advertising is Communication

Communication is a fashionable word today. It simply means talking to people. This is what advertising does. It talks to people. To be effective, therefore, it must talk to them in the *language it understands*.

Such language will vary from audience to audience. With a group of well educated people the copywriter can employ the words and phrases he is likely to use in his or her everyday life. On the other hand, with a working class audience, more simple and direct words are essential. Nothing symbolises communication-failure more than to witness the hostile or satirical reactions of a down-to-earth group of working people to a television commercial which employs Mayfair voices and situations in the wrong context. Equally, with such an audience, the determined 'by Gum' approach is also likely to fail. People in all walks of life have a strong instinct for the false note in advertising—or in anything else. They know perfectly well when the language is the wrong language. Fortunately, there is growing realisation of this fact in advertising. More attention is being paid to the importance of saying things in the right way to the people to whom one is selling. At long last, it seems, margarine advertisers have caught up with the fact that most people in this country use the soft 'g' in margarine.

Following on from this, it is also important for an advertising message to be *sincere.* No doubt all of you are familiar with the foot-in-the-door salesman who rattles off his patter nineteen to the dozen. You are probably also familiar with advertisements which do the same thing, with a plentiful supply of jargon thrown in for good measure. This kind of approach is likely to be dismissed out of hand. Advertising is talking to people, not bombarding them with endless superlatives which no one believes. Nor are people very willing to believe the opposite approach, the one based on 'let us be your friend', usually uttered (on TV at any rate) in a treacly voice, dripping over with false bonhomie or understanding. Again, people have an instinct about these things. But what they will respond to is sincerity. A good example of this is the Home Pride Flour campaign. The product has a plus, but instead of dealing in mysterious magic ingredients the agency (Geers Gross) devised cartoon-figures to put over the selling points with humour and charm. This advertising is eminently believable not only because of the sheer creative skill with which the 'finer flour' story is promoted but also because of its absolute sincerity (i.e., believability).

The Home Pride campaign also demonstrates another important principle: make the proposition instantly *understandable.* In advertising, as in any form of communication, it is vitally important that your audience understands what you are trying to tell it. It is all too easy to project an advertising message based on knowledge which the company and the agency has about the product, and to overlook the fact that the consumer does not necessarily have this knowledge. It is all too easy to be brief (which in principle is desirable) to the point of being ambiguous or incoherent (which is not!). It is all too easy in the search to be 'different' to create a proposition which is obscure or which says the wrong things. In Chapter 10 you will see that the modern advertiser (rightly) sets a great deal of store on checking whether his proposed advertising message is comprehensible. If it is not, then communication breaks down and the advertising is wasted if it is allowed to appear.

As in any form of communication, it is important too for the advertiser to achieve *identity*. It is an old, but valid, device to take a number of advertisements covering products in the same market and to eliminate the logotypes (i.e., the name-plates). Very often the advertising of one competitor cannot be distingushed from another. Yet who could associate the Chimpanzees in the television advertisements with anyone else but Brooke Bond? Here the agency (Davidson, Pearce, Berry & Spottiswoode) has achieved a unique means of identifying the brand and the company—as well as an effective selling device. The same is true of Anadin advertising. This cannot be confused with the advertising for any other headache remedy. Everyone concerned with creating advertisements should strive for *identity*, for individual personality, otherwise there is a danger that they will merge into an undistinguishable mass.

Finally, it is important to bear in mind that in advertising what is communicated has a cumulative effect. It creates an attitude in the mind of the consumer known as the *brand-image*. This is not jargon but a convenient way of summing up what people *feel* about a brand. Such a feeling is developed not only by the advertising for that brand but also through packaging and all the other elements of the marketing mix. Nevertheless, advertising is probably the biggest single influence and it pays to bear this in mind at all times. In the life of a brand, there may be many advertising campaigns to exploit new situations, or even new markets. However, none of these campaigns should be conceived in a vacuum. Each new one should be assessed against the brand image to see whether it consolidates it or militates against it. The exigencies of a given situation should never be allowed to alter the brand image unless such a step is taken consciously in respect of new needs or requirements. A favourable image is a priceless asset which has to be protected. Bear in mind, therefore, that every advertisement published is an investment in the brand. It is imperative to make certain that a good investment is made each time.

FOR FURTHER READING

Techniques of Persuasion (J. A. C. Brown, Penguin Books Ltd.).

Psychology: the Science of Mental Life (G. A. Miller, Hutchinson Publishing Group Ltd.).

The Psychology of Perception (M. D. Vernon, University of London Press).

Attitude Formation and Change (J. D. Halloran, Leicester University Press).

Effective Advertising Copy Merrill (De Voe, Collier MacMillan Ltd.).

Copywriting (P. Stobo, Business Books Ltd. for I.P.A.).

Advertising Layout and Art Direction (S. Baker, McGraw-Hill Publishing Ltd.).

The Typography of Press Advertisement (K. Day, Ernest Benn Ltd.).

Processes of Graphic Reproduction in Printing (H. Curwen, Faber & Faber Ltd.).

The Preparation of Colour Artwork (I.P.A. publication).

CHAPTER EIGHT

Delivering the Advertising Message

MAJOR MEDIA FOR ADVERTISING: CATEGORIES AND CHARACTERISTICS

In its literal sense the word *media* (which is the plural for *medium*) can be used to describe the outlet for any means of communication, e.g., book-match covers and beer mats. However, in advertising it is more commonly applied to major vehicles of communication:

Press, Television, Outdoor, Cinema, Radio, Direct Mail

and it is these we will be considering in this chapter.

There is no such thing as a 'best' medium, in absolute terms. Each medium has advantages and disadvantages, and the choice for advertising purposes is determined by the requirements of an individual project. In principle, it is better to use *one* medium adequately than to use a variety of media inadequately. Thus most campaigns major on one medium, with other media, if employed at all, used in a supporting role.

THE PRESS

This is a generic word which covers a vast range of printed newspapers and magazines. (Sometimes the press is called the PRINT medium.) The main sub-divisions are:

National Daily Press

Because of Britain's size and compactness, it is unique in having genuinely *national* newspapers which can reach almost everyone in all parts of the country by breakfast time each day. Most people buy or read a national daily newspaper (the majority, of course, are delivered) and such media, in combination, can achieve around 85% coverage of the adult population. For the national advertiser this is a tremendous asset, especially since the costs of reaching such a vast audience are relatively low. In addition to near-blanket coverage, the national dailies provide an advertising vehicle which ensures authoritative and urgent exposure of the advertising message.

Of course, the national press can be used more selectively. For example, if upper-income readers are the target, there are sufficient quality newspapers to provide high and economical coverage of these people. The growth of special regional editions of national newspapers also enables the advertiser to use them to cover certain *areas*, if, for one reason or another, he does not require national coverage (e.g., in test marketing, see Chapter 3, or split-run copy testing, see Chapter 10).

Another facility which is being made increasingly available to advertisers is the use of *colour*. This is possible because of printing and paper-making developments, the results of which create the opportunity in a newspaper format to add the sales appeal of full-colour previously only possible with magazines.

National Sunday Newspapers

These also achieve high coverage of the population. With the right combination, up to 90% can be reached; thus, like the dailies, the Sundays provide the opportunity for wide exposure of the advertising message. Since they are usually read when more leisure time is available, they offer a potentially deep exposure, i.e., the Sundays are studied thoroughly. They also provide a large measure of selectivity in that they can be used to reach given audiences across the social scale.

General National Magazines

These are few in number but high in coverage. For example, the Radio Times and TV Times between them reach 35% of the adult population. Reader's Digest is another widely read publication with high readership. (Each has special regional editions.) Other popular magazines include Tit-Bits, Weekend, Reveille and Thomson's Weekly News. Publications of this kind enable advertisers to reach large audiences at very economical rates. Magazines lack the immediacy of the press but have the advantage of a longer life and thus provide potentially longer advertising exposure.

National Women's Magazines

Magazines which appeal directly to women are very popular in Britain. The four leading mass circulation magazines are Woman, Woman's Own, Woman's Realm and Woman's Weekly, which between them reach 60% of the female population. Their appeal tends to be universal, that is they are largely classless and thus they are a very efficient and economical means of reaching a large number of women and girls in all age and class groups. In addition to these publications there are a large number of women's magazines geared to specific interest and class groups, e.g., beauty, fashion, domestic, mothercraft and 'teenage' magazines. The editorial format of women's magazines provides a very suitable framework for advertising to women and this is a major advantage to many advertisers; they also have a relatively long life.

Provincial Press

There are more than 1,000 provincial newspapers in Britain. They divide into 5 categories:

Mornings. These are few in number and are concentrated in major cities. The Birmingham Post, Glasgow Herald, Edinburgh Scotsman and the Plymouth Western Morning News are typical examples. They tend to be 'quality' newpapers with a strong business and social flavour and are an ideal vehicle for advertisers who wish to supplement their advertising in the national 'quality' newspapers.

Provincial Sundays. A few major cities, such as Glasgow, Newcastle and Birmingham provide a local Sunday newspaper. Such newspapers have a strong popular appeal, on the lines of the People rather than the Sunday Times, and offer extremely good local coverage.

Provincial Evenings. These are by far the biggest element in the provincial press structure. Almost every town[1] of any size has an evening news-

[1] London has two newspapers, the *News* and *Standard.* These are usually classified as semi-national newspapers since their circulation and coverage extends over most of the Home Counties as well as London.

paper. The coverage of most 'evenings' is extremely high and in some towns approaches the 100% level. This is to say that nearly every household in those towns buys or reads the 'local' paper, which tends to be read by the whole family. Thus, provincial evenings are a valuable asset to the local advertiser and also have an important role to play for many national advertisers.

Suburban and Provincial Weeklies. In the London Suburbs, Home Counties and throughout Britain, there are a large number of weekly newspapers. These tend to concentrate entirely on local news, as distinct from the three categories already mentioned, which feature national and world news as well. Their strong local bias makes them a natural for local advertisers, but they are also used by national advertisers, particularly in tie-ups with local stores, and by Government Departments and Nationalised industries (e.g., Gas and Electricity Boards). Such publications have a long life, are read in depth and at leisure, and achieve high advertising exposure among their readers.

'Give-aways'. These are a growing feature of the provincial press scene. Such newspapers are produced by a number of companies (some of them already in the 'conventional' newspaper business) and distributed house to house on a virtual saturation basis. No charge is made to the reader, the publisher deriving his revenue entirely from advertisers. This development has achieved widespread succes in the U.S.A. and, despite a number of early failures (inevitable at the teething stage), is showing every sign of becoming a significant factor in Britain.

Specialist Consumer Publications

Britain is rich in magazines which cater for a wide range of special interests from Angling to Zoology. Thus any advertiser who wishes to reach a given audience can usually find a suitable vehicle in which to expose his message, either exclusively or as a supporting medium for more general publications.

Professional, Trade and Technical Press

There are a wide range of publications covering individual professions, trades and industries. For example, the manufacturer who sells through chemists has three pharmacy trade journals which he can use in order to influence the distribution and sale of his products. Similarly, a manufacturer selling machine tools has a number of journals available capable of reaching buyers in all sectors of industry.

COMMERCIAL TELEVISION

Commercial television reaches[1] 17 million homes out of a total of 18·4 million homes in Britain. Thus nearly 90% of all households have television sets capable of receiving I.T.V. programmes. Commercial television's share of total viewership has consistently been in excess of 50% over the past 10 years. Where this medium is concerned, therefore, advertisers have the means of reaching mass audiences both on a national and a regional scale.

These are the programme companies which comprise the complete television network (each with I.T.A. contracts up to 1976). They are:

London (Weekday)	Thames Television Ltd.
London (Weekend)	London Weekend Television Ltd.
Midlands	A.T.V. Network Ltd.
Lancashire	Granada Television Ltd.
Yorkshire North East	Trident Management Ltd.
Central Scotland N.East Scotland	Scottish Television & Grampian Sales Ltd.
Wales and the West	Harlech Television Ltd.

[1] Source: British Bureau of Television Advertising.

Map of ITV Regions
(Reproduced by courtesy of British Bureau of Television Advertising Ltd. and Audits of Great Britain Ltd.)

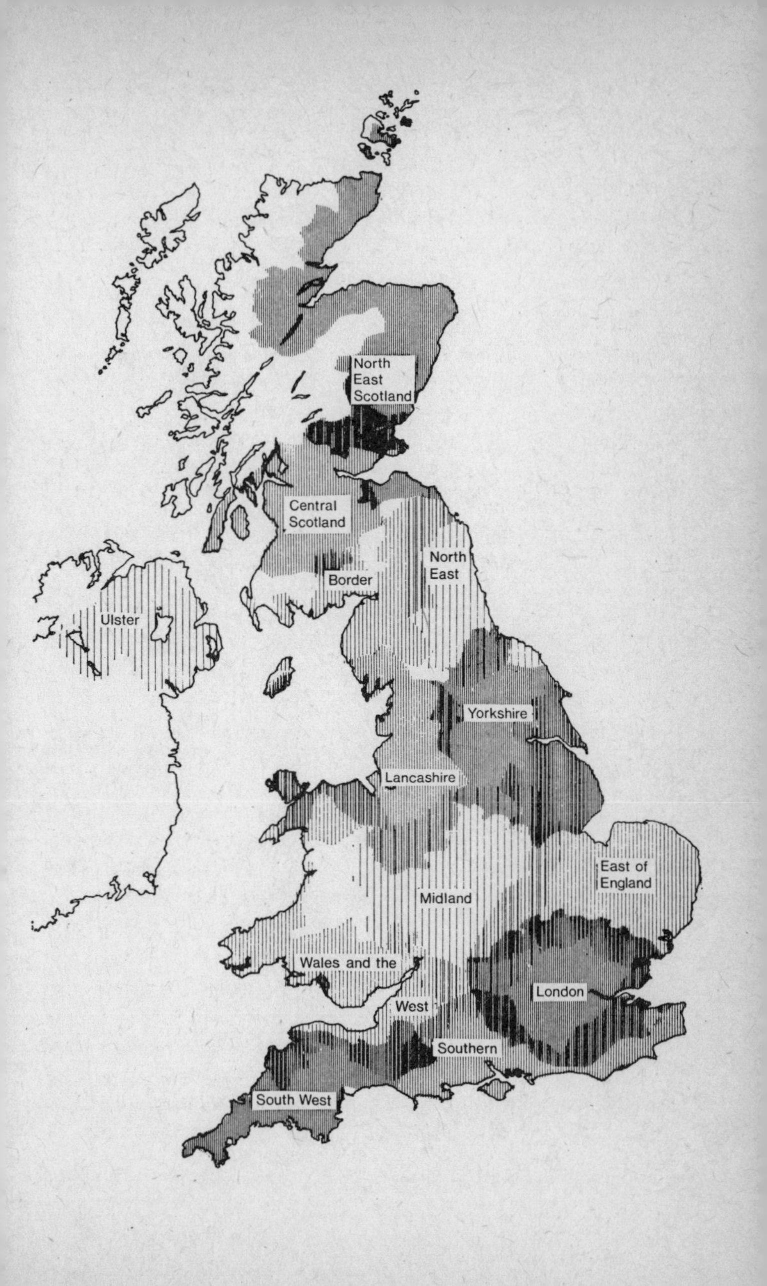
North
East
Scotland
Central
Scotland
Border
North
East
Ulster
Yorkshire
Lancashire
East of
England
Midland
Wales and the
West
London
Southern
South West

Southern	Southern Television Ltd.
East of England	Anglia Television Ltd.
Ulster	Ulster Television Ltd.
South West	Westward Television Ltd.
Border	Border Television Ltd.
Channel Islands	Channel Television Ltd.

The advantages of commercial television for the advertiser are that it provides broad scale and flexible (i.e., national and regional) coverage, plus a vehicle which enables him to *dramatise* and *demonstrate* his proposition in the viewer's own home. Television adds the dimension of movement and sound to advertising and these have proved to be extremely effective for many advertisers. The advent of *colour television* adds yet another asset to this medium, although it is likely to be some years before there is a mass-ownership of the necessary receivers.

OUTDOOR

The range of media available to the advertiser in this area is considerable, despite the fact that all outdoor advertising is subject to considerable restrictions under the TOWN AND COUNTRY PLANNING ACT 1947. This Act gives both national and local Government extensive powers to control and regulate the placing and use of sites. Here are the main categories:

Posters

These are sited on approved hoardings in shopping centres, open ground, on football and atheletic grounds, and in a variety of places where prominence can be achieved together with big audience exposure.

A feature of the post war outdoor advertising scene is the *Bulletin Board*. Such sites have been developed to provide advertisers with a strong and dominant advertising vehicle while still preserving local amenity.

The advantages of poster advertising lie in its capacity to project a product name and proposition in a very direct and easy to assimilate way, frequently close to the point of sale. Good audience coverage is possible and, of course, a high degree of flexibility in that a poster campaign can be used nationally, regionally or even locally.

Transport

The siting of *posters* in varying sizes is a common feature of Railway and Underground stations. In addition, however, there are a variety of other outlets for advertising. *Bus sides* and *Bus backs* are widely available for both London and Provincial buses. Many bus companies also provide advertising space on the inside of buses. The *Escalator Cards* of the London Underground system are famous (notably for foundation garment advertising!) and another well used vehicle for advertisers are *Car Cards* in the tube trains themselves.

All these media are quite obviously able to offer the advertiser good coverage given the density of population movement in busy urban centres. Thus advertisements in transport media achieve a high exposure rate.

Pictorial Signs

Nearly everyone is familiar with the pictorial signs at Piccadilly Circus in London and in other major cities. Some are static advertisements, but many incorporate some kind of 'movement' to add interest and to achieve greater impact. Such advertisements can scarcely be missed but, even so, some advertisers seek to command viewership by providing an in-built service to the public. A good example of this is the Guinness clock in Piccadilly Circus, London. Another example is the *Newscaster* device. Newscasters feature the news, interspersed with advertisements at regular intervals, thus ensuring *specific* audience attention.

When pictorial signs were first introduced towards the beginning of this century, following the discovery of neon gas, they were considered to be vulgar. Now, however, they are essentially prestige media. A brand big enough and important enough to be featured 'in lights' is generally regarded as having 'arrived'.

CINEMA

The changing social scene, notably the advent of television, has drastically reduced the cinema-going habit. In 1948, 37 million admission tickets were sold each week. In 1971 the total was 3·5 million. Nevertheless, this is still a sizeable audience and moreover has the merit of being well-defined. The majority of cinema-goers today are young men and women 16–24, many of whom enjoy a fair degree of affluence. Therefore, they constitute a valuable market for a number of advertisers, notably those in the cosmetic, toiletry, confectionery, ice cream, cigarette and mineral water fields. Local advertisers also use the cinema extensively to promote restaurants, garages, laundry and dry cleaning services, job vacancies, and many other goods and services.

Cinema advertising, like television advertising, offers movement and sound and also the added dimension of colour. Thus, it is possible to achieve considerable impact and memorability on film with high national, regional or even local flexibility. With many goods (e.g., ice cream and confectionery) advertising can be directly linked with on-the-spot sales. It can also be linked with feature films themselves and many successful tie-ups have been achieved by such *cross promotion.*

RADIO

Since the collapse of the 'Pirate' radio stations, the only significant medium for radio advertising to British audiences is *Radio Luxembourg.* This has been available for many years and despite competition from three television and four (B.B.C.) radio channels, it still commands good audiences for its evening transmissions. Listeners are heavily biased towards the younger age groups and most of the comments made in relation to cinema advertising are also applicable here, in terms of the product and services which are promoted therein.

Commercial Radio on a big scale will be established in 1973/4 under the auspices of the Independent Broadcasting Authority (which will also control independent television). The plan calls for radio stations numbering up to 80, serving audiences on a local basis throughout the main conurbations. The transmission pattern is likely to provide day-time as well as evening broadcasting and thus a wide spectrum of audience coverage.

Experience in radio advertising is confined to a relatively small number of personnel in Britain, since this medium has not been available except in a fairly limited way. However, those who have used it know that it can

FRUIT (contd.)	
& Vegetable Canners	305
& Vegetable Growers	10,000
& Vegetable Merchants—Wholesale	4,400
FRUITERERS & GREENGROCERS—RETAIL	17,000
FRUITERERS & GREENGROCERS—RETAIL—CO-OPERATIVE HEAD OFFICES	735
FUNERAL DIRECTORS	3,250
FUR & SKIN MERCHANTS	430
FURNACE & OVEN BUILDERS	380
FURNISHING FABRICS MANUFACTURERS	270
FURNITURE	
Designers	210
Manufacturers & Cabinet Makers	3,600
Removers & Storers	2,800
Retailers—Leading	5,000
Retailers—Co-operative Head Offices	800
Tubular Steel—Manufacturers	85
FURRIERS—MANUFACTURING	520
FURRIERS—RETAIL	1,400
FUSE & FUSE BOX MANUFACTURERS	50

g

GALVANIZED HOLLOWARE MANUFACTURERS	120
GALVANIZERS	65
GAMES MANUFACTURERS	120
GARAGE EQUIPMENT & TOOLS MANUFACTURERS	55
GARAGES & FILLING STATIONS	32,000
GARAGES—WITH REPAIR FACILITIES	22,600
GARDEN	
Furniture & Appliance Manufacturers	85
Ornament Manufacturers	65
Supplies Retailers	8,500
Tool Manufacturers	40
GARDENERS—LANDSCAPE	740
GARDENERS—MARKET	6,000
GARDENS—ZOOLOGICAL	20
GAS	
Compressor Manufacturers	45
Cookers—Manufacturers	20
Council—Area Boards	10
Council—Divisions & Groups	115
Council—Local Offices & Showrooms	1,300
Engine Manufacturers	45
Holder Stations	250

35

This is an extract from a brochure issued by a leading direct mail house. The brochure enumerates the number of prospects which the company's mailing list can reach over a wide range of categories
(Reproduced by courtesy of Advance Direct Mail Service Ltd.)

be a very effective medium. It reaches what is known as a captive audience with a message which can be selected to match the mood of the immediate programme context. Thus it can be both persuasive and urgent, and, used in the right way, radio advertising has the capacity to evoke considerable audience response.

DIRECT MAIL

Direct mail means *advertising* through the post (it is not to be confused with mail order which is *selling* through the post, usually via the initial vehicle of press advertising). Thus, instead of the advertising message being conveyed in a newspaper or magazine, or by the television screen, it is actually directed through the letter box of the recipient.

In some text books on advertising, you will find that direct mail is referred to as an ancillary medium. This is not entirely true. In terms of the expenditure involved, direct mail is the *third* biggest medium and one which is expanding rapidly.

Until fairly recently, postal advertising was confined largely to well-defined specialist audiences, e.g., retailers, doctors, architects, etc. While such people still receive a large percentage of all mailing that is sent out, the use of direct mail to the general public is increasing rapidly, notably in connection with book and long-playing record clubs. Names and addresses are obtained through a variety of means: the electoral register, membership lists of professional bodies; they are also built up from manufacturers and department stores' own files (e.g., from requests for information or, where the latter are concerned, from purchases made at those shops).

The advantages of direct mail lie in its accuracy, that is to say a given section of people (i.e., sales prospects) can be pin-pointed precisely. Consequently, there is potentially less waste circulation. Direct mail also has immediacy and can be a very potent sales-builder. This underlines another advantage: that the medium lends itself to the specific and immediate selling proposition (bearing in mind also that it provides a convenient means of response, e.g., usually a reply-paid card), thus it is frequently possible to measure results against expenditure.

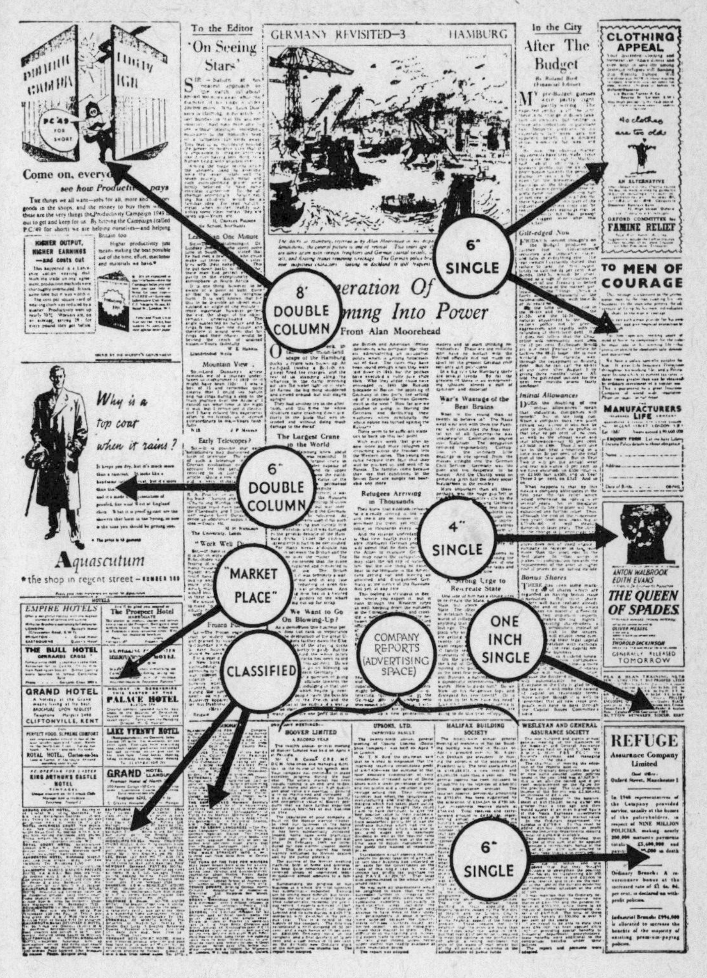

To the Editor

'On Seeing Stars'

GERMANY REVISITED—3 HAMBURG

In the City

After The Budget

Come on, everyo...

see how Productiv... pays

HIGHER OUTPUT, HIGHER EARNINGS —and costs cut

CLOTHING APPEAL

No clothes are too old

OXFORD COMMITTEE for FAMINE RELIEF

TO MEN OF COURAGE

MANUFACTURERS LIFE

Mountain View

Early Telescopes?

The Largest Crane in the World

Refugees Arriving in Thousands

War's Wastage of the Best Brains

Gilt-edged Now

Initial Allowances

Bonus Shares

We Want to Go On Blowing-Up?

Why is a top coat when it rains?

Aquascutum

the shop in regent street

ANTON WALBROOK

EDITH EVANS

THE QUEEN OF SPADES

GENERALLY RELEASED TOMORROW

EMPIRE HOTELS

The Prospect Hotel

THE BULL HOTEL

GRAND HOTEL

CLIFTONVILLE, KENT

PALACE HOTEL

LAKE VYRNWY HOTEL

KING ARTHUR'S CASTLE HOTEL

HOOVER LIMITED

UPSONS, LTD.

HALIFAX BUILDING SOCIETY

WESLEYAN AND GENERAL ASSURANCE SOCIETY

REFUGE Assurance Company Limited

A page from a leading newspaper, showing various types and sizes of press advertisement

However, direct mail is expensive, more so than any other medium in terms of relative costs. It calls for specialised skills to overcome the apathy or actual resistance to postal advertising which some people possess. These skills embrace the use of personalised letters[1] and a range of other techniques; those wishing to use this medium are advised to seek expert advice from a company specialising in this form of advertising.

THE ADVERTISING MESSAGE: SIZE AND TIME UNITS, SPECIMEN RATES

The Press

For newspapers of all kinds, nationals and provincials, the basic unit of advertising space is calculated and made available in terms of the *single column inch* (s.c.i.). This a 1″ single is an advertisement 1 inch deep × 1 column wide. Actually, such a space is rare and the most common space units are those indicated on the diagram on page 87.

Newspaper advertisement rates are quoted on a s.c.i. basis and, like all rates, are geared to circulation. Thus if £30 is the basic rate per s.c.i., a 6″ × 2 columns (12 units in all) would cost £360. All newspapers charge extra rates for spaces which are *solus* (no other advertising on the page) or *next matter* (immediately next to editorial matter). The generic description for such spaces is *special positions* while ordinary positions are referred to as *run of paper* (R.O.P.).

Advertising space-costs in magazines are calculated in relation to *one full page* and proportions thereof. The most common range of sizes is $\frac{1}{8}$th page, $\frac{1}{4}$ page, $\frac{1}{2}$ page and 1 page. (Rates are seldom *pro rata* in popular magazines, that is a half-page will usually be more than half the cost of a full page and so on.) Most magazines, like newspapers, offer *special* positions at higher rates. Similarly, colour is more expensive than monochrome.

[1] A duplicated letter printed in such a way that it appears to have been addressed personally to the recipient.

Some Examples of Press Rates

Circulation and total readership figures are also included for comparison.

	Whole page monochrome	*Circulation*[1]	*Total readers*[1]
National Daily Newspapers	£		
Daily Express	5,500	3,390,049	9,705,000
Daily Mirror	3,998	4,388,446	13,767,000
The Times	2,640	338,653	1,066,000
National Sunday Newspapers			
News of the World	8,448	6,085,680	15,840,000
Sunday Mirror	4,032	4,677,999	13,517,000
Observer	3,696	802,268	2,378,000
General and Women's Magazines			
T.V. Times	2,650	3,202,645	9,852,000
Woman	2,830	2,005,074	7,991,000
Nova	440	109,210	912,000
Provincial Newspapers			
Newcastle Sunday Sun	792	209,825	—
Manchester Evening News	1,550	406,157	961,000
Edinburgh Scotsman	720	75,065	—
Kenilworth Weekly News	44	4,207	—

Television

Sponsored television programmes are forbidden by the Television Act 1954. Therefore, all advertisements have to be transmitted by means of filmed commercials, slotted into programmes during 'natural breaks'. No more than 7 minutes of advertising per hour is allowed.

Advertisers may buy time segments (usually called *spots*) out of the time available. Spots are standard units of 60, 45, 30, 15 and 7 seconds. Rates are fixed in accordance with the time required. *Peak spots* (when the viewing audience is large, i.e., in the evening) are naturally more

[1]Sources: Audit Bureau of Circulation, July–December 1971; JICTARS National Readership Survey, January–December 1971.

This is a still from a Brooke Bond P.G. Tips TV commercial, featuring the celebrated chimps. The use of these attractive animals has enabled the advertiser to entertain the consumer and yet build sales at the same time. The chimps achieve instant brand-identification, a high degree of consumer awareness and are an important means of engendering consumer goodwill. Note that their actions are always relevant to the use of the product, which is never lost sight of despite the unusual nature of this advertising approach
(Reproduced by courtesy of Brooke Bond Oxo Ltd. Agency: Davidson, Pearce, Berry & Spottiswoode Ltd.)

A scene from the 1970 Advertising Association annual conference. This is an occasion when all sections of the industry get together to discuss industry problems and also wider social and economic issues
(Photograph by courtesy of the Advertising Association)

One of the most striking forms of outdoor advertising is the Bulletin Board, reproduced here
(Photographs by courtesy of Cosales, the U.K. Consortium of Outdoor Advertising)

Cinemas still attract large audiences each week. Illustrated here is a typical, modern suburban cinema—the ABC at Edgware, Middlesex
(Photograph by courtesy of Associated British Cinemas Ltd. and Pearl & Dean Ltd.)

Radio Luxembourg reaches a predominantly young audience. Featured here are four of its leading disc jockeys
(Photograph by courtesy of Radio Luxembourg)

These are examples of gifts available through Green Shield Stamps. The total range of gifts offered to stamp savers by this company numbers almost 1400
(Photograph by courtesy of Green Shield Trading Stamp Co. Ltd.)

Another example of how sales promotion can be linked with advertising. Here is a Brooke Bond chimp photographed with children at the opening of a new supermarket in the west country. These chimps are widely used on such occasions since they help to sell tea for Brooke Bond and increase traffic for the participating store
(Photograph by courtesy of Brooke Bond Oxo Ltd. Agency: Davidson, Pearce, Berry & Spottiswoode Ltd.)

PG
TIPS

SPEND THE DAY AT LONGLEAT *
WARMINSTER
WILTSHIRE
* BRITAIN'S FIRST BIG-GAME RESERVE

things go better with Coke
Coca-Cola

Del Monte
SLICED PINEAPPLE

Del Monte
peel a can today

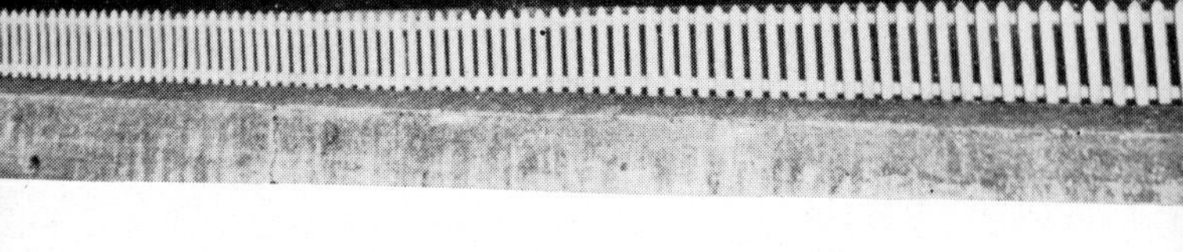

DIPLOMAT
the sporting cigarette

ABC
GALA CHARITY OPENING TONIGHT AT 7.15
WAIT UNTIL DARK
CONTINUOUS FROM SUNDAY
OPTICIAN

DAVID CHRISTIAN

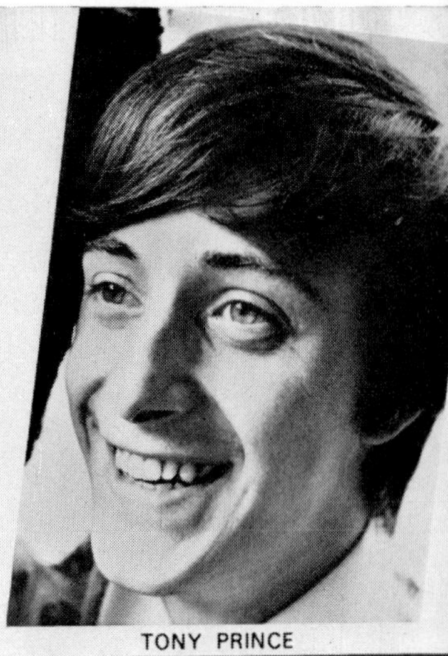

TONY PRINCE

BOB STEWART

PAUL BURNETT

208 PEOPLE
YOUR LUXEMBOURG D.J.'s

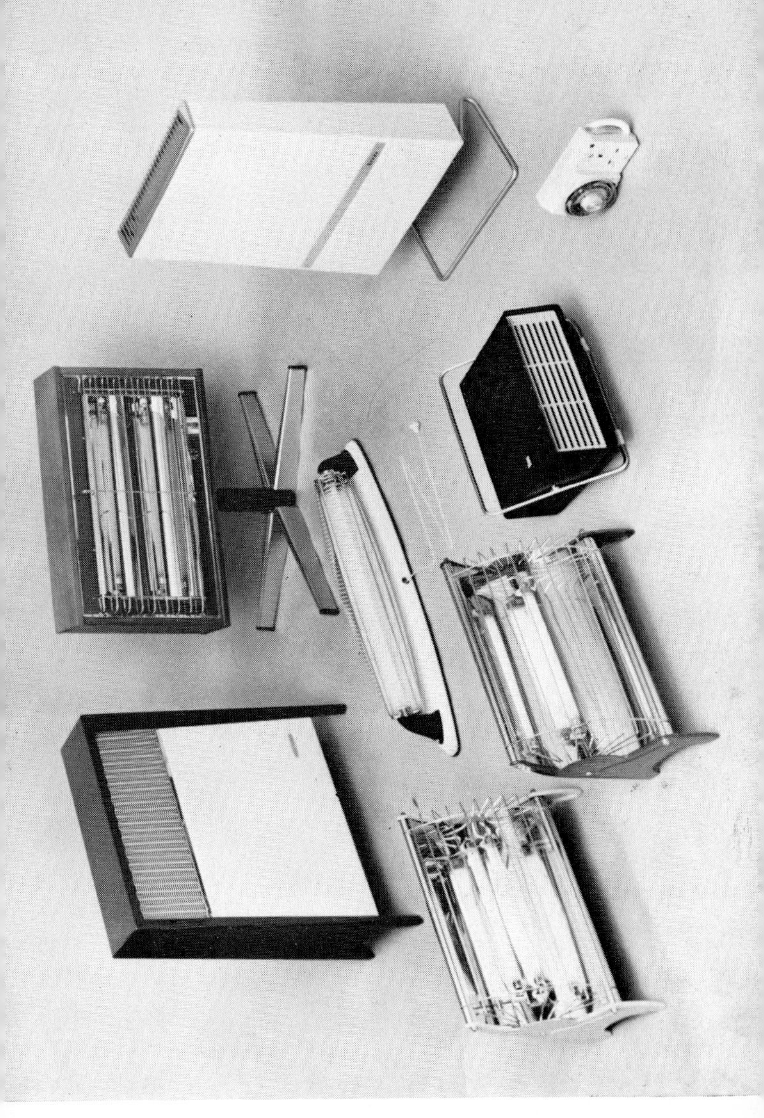

expensive than *off-peak spots* (afternoon, early or late evening when the audience is lower). In the summer, when television viewing is lighter, special bonuses are offered to advertisers to compensate for lower audiences.

Some Examples of Television Rates

Station	*Cost of 30 sec peak £*	*Total ITV homes*	*Average no. of homes viewing in peak*
London (Thames)	1,600	4,160,000	1,290,000
Midlands	800	2,620,000	790,000
Central Scotland	330	1,175,000	330,000
Ulster	105	356,000	110,000

Outdoor (Posters only)

Posters are available in a range of standard sizes:

	Depth	*Width*
Double Crown	30″ ×	20″
4 sheet	5′ ×	20″
16 sheet	10′ ×	6′ 8″
32 sheet	10′ ×	13′ 4″
48 sheet	10′ ×	20′
Bulletin Board	9′6″ ×	27′

Bulletin Boards can also be 36′ and 45′ wide.
Rates vary considerably and hinge upon the position of the site.

Cinema

Two types of advertising units may be bought:
 Slides of 15 seconds.
 Commercials of 120 seconds, 60 seconds, 30 seconds and 15 seconds.

Radio

Spots on Radio Luxembourg may be bought in the following lengths:
 60, 45, 30, 15 and 7 seconds.

Note: It is not feasible to provide examples of rates for cinema or radio since, like posters, they are infinitely variable.

Direct Mail

The use of a mailing list issued by a company specialising in direct mail (a mailing house) is usually charged on the basis of a payment per 1,000 respondents. The actual charge will depend upon the importance of the list.

Note: All advertising rates quoted are those obtaining in January 1970. Please bear in mind that these may quickly become out of date.

PRINCIPLES OF MEDIA PLANNING

(A) *Media Planning Task*

This is to:

Deliver the advertising message to the greatest number of prospects as often as possible at the right time in the most suitable environment at the lowest possible cost.

This task embodies four distinct elements:

COVERAGE

REPETITION

CREATIVELY SUITABLE ENVIRONMENT

TIMING AND DURATION

and, as we will see, involves not only the use and interpretation of statistical data but also the need to harmonise such data with creative factors.

Coverage

For most markets, consumer/trade/industrial, there are media which are read or seen by large numbers of prospects. Reaching these prospects is called *coverage* and the media planner has to decide, in relation to the target audience and the money he has, what coverage he can obtain of those prospects. He will usually seek very high coverage, for obvious reasons, and most media planners will not settle for less than 80%

coverage of a given market. It may be asked why the figure is not nearer 100%. There are two reasons. First, there are always a percentage of people who do not read newspapers, or magazines, or watch television. Thus it is virtually impossible to reach everyone. The second reason is concerned with *cost.*

Media planning involves the projected expenditure of money. Quite frequently, the sums of money are very large indeed, but, regardless of the amount, the same care has to be taken as in any other area of commerce to achieve the greatest possible efficiency per £ spent. In other words, to ensure value for money.

Here are two simple examples in press media planning to demonstrate the point. *Coverage* of a given market can usually be obtained in a variety of ways. The media planner has to select the media which provide the most economical coverage. Now the basic unit of cost measurement in media planning is *cost per 1,000*; this is calculated by correlating the readership or circulation of each medium with the space rates charged. This means that each medium can then be cost-evaluated by the same criterion. To obtain coverage, it is necessary to study various media combinations, to see which combination delivers the desired audience at the lowest cost.

Let us assume the national press is the chosen medium.

Media Combination 1

Schedule based on Papers A, B, C, D = 80% coverage of target audience

Cost = 105 (Index Basis).

Media Combination 2

Schedule based on Papers B, C, D, E = 80% coverage of target audience

Cost = 100 (Index Basis).

Clearly the second combination is the more economical, although it is emphasised that other combinations will be examined. Please bear in mind also that the papers within a given combination must satisfy the media planner's other requirements, e.g., they must be creatively suitable.

Not only is this method used to establish basic coverage but also *optimum* coverage; this means there is usually a cut-off point beyond which it is too costly to obtain additional coverage. The following example is taken from a real life situation:

Existing Schedule (A). Target Audience A, B, C1 (higher socio-economic groups).

Media Combination: G, H, I, J, K, L, M = 84% coverage
Cost = 110 (Index Basis).

New Schedule based on optimised coverage (B). Same target audience.

Media Combination: G, H, I, J, K = 80% coverage.
Cost = 100 (Index basis).

Schedule A delivers 4% extra coverage but at 10% higher cost. Other media combinations showed that to get beyond 80% coverage also increased costs above an acceptable level and thus Schedule B was the one selected.

Repetition

The consumer's attention is constantly being sought from a wide range of sources, not least that from other advertisers; therefore, to make any impression with an individual campaign it is nescessary to expose the advertising message as frequently as possible. This is called *repetition.*

Repetition is achieved by seeing that the advertising message is inserted on the screen, or in each publication selected, frequently during the campaign. This means that viewers or readers will get the opportunity of seeing it on a number of occasions. So far as the major press media (national newspapers and magazines) are concerned, however, there is another source of repetition and the media planner will take this into account when constructing his plan. This derives from the fact that many people read more than one paper or magazine. Such readership is called *duplication* and this can be a valuable asset not only because it ensures bonus repetition but also because it provides the opportunity, if required, for economies in space buying. For example, the number of insertions in each publication can be reduced if the degree of repetition required is achieved by using an appropriate combination of publications (provided, of course, coverage targets are also achieved). The concept of repetition in major press media planning is called *opportunities to see* (O.T.S.) and can be calculated in advance. Such refined techniques are not possible with television, since it is a universal medium (whereas the press sub-divides into a number of sectional groups).

One important point. So far as repetition in an individual medium is concerned, this is not just a matter of making the advertisement as small or as short as possible. By concentrating on low-priced 1″ × 1 column advertisements in the press, or 7 second commercials on television, the media planner could afford tremendous frequency (repetition) even with a relatively small appropriation. However, there are few propositions which can be expressed adequately in such limited space or time and this is one instance out of many when the media planner has to take into account the creative requirements as well as statistics. He has to balance the need for repetition with the need for advertisements of sufficient space and time to do justice to the proposition.

Creatively Suitable Environment

This is a way of saying that the advertising message must be exposed in a setting which is suitable for the product proposition. At its most elementary this means that a media planner would not use the sports pages of a newspaper (which are read largely by men) to advertise a product for women. He would clearly dictate that it appears in the woman's section or at any rate in a section of the paper in which there is high woman readership.

However, this concept extends far beyond this obvious example and embraces not merely the use of a given medium but indeed its *selection.* For example, on pure statistics (selective coverage, costs, etc.) the priority medium for a given proposition could be the national press. But the advertising proposition might well hinge on the dramatic demonstration of the product to the consumer. This could point the way to television, the ideal medium for demonstration, and therefore, provided the planner has the resources to plan a *viable TV* campaign, he may, in this instance, give precedence to the creative requirement. This underlines once again the fact that media planning is more than statistics, important though they are.

Timing and Duration

Timing has already been discussed in Chapter 5 and, if the campaign planning team has done its job properly, the media planner will not only be well briefed on the timing and duration of the campaign but will also be able to ensure that the plan can be drawn up in time to meet the deadlines. (Note: Magazines can go to press any time up to 3 months before publication; this must be taken into account if they are to be used.)

So far as the duration of the campaign is concerned, this obviously depends upon product and market characteristics, although money availability may also be a determining factor, e.g., on a limited budget it may be better to have a strong, short campaign rather than attempt to spread the butter too thinly over a long period. In markets where purchasing is on a regular basis throughout the year (e.g., tea, bread, toothpaste) there is a case for running the campaign on a twelve months basis if funds permit. On the other hand, even big advertisers may prefer a burst pattern rather than the steady drip-drip approach and there are no hard and fast rules. Seasonality, of course, has a big influence. With products sold predominantly in the winter months (e.g., canned soups) the weight of advertising will clearly be applied at this time and an advertising campaign here will probably be based on a September-March duration (with a possible separate lighter weight campaign promoting summer use during the April-August period).

(B) *Media Planning Controls*

These are the factors which the media planner must establish before he can undertake his task.

Appropriation. Clearly he must know how much money is available.

Target audience. Again he must know which audience the advertising message is to be aimed at.

Product and market characteristics. It is essential for him to understand the product and its uses in relation to the market in which it is being sold. How much is the product? Is it bought frequently or infrequently? Is it bought predominantly on Friday or Saturday? (As many food products are.) Is it bought throughout the year or mainly in one period of the year? Is it used exclusively by women or is it a family product? This information will help to determine the advertising pattern to be established.

Timing and duration. This follows from the foregoing, but must be defined clearly in order that planning can be carried out within the right time and length framework.

Creative requirements. The media planner must liaise with creative personnel to ensure that *creative* requirements are met. If a press campaign has been decided, can the advertising proposition be expressed in smaller spaces or does it require larger spaces? If the latter, what size and shape of space is likely to be wanted? If a television campaign has been decided, what length of spot is needed to get the message across? The important consideration here is to ensure that the media planner is not divorced from the creative operation. The days when media plans were devised in isolation, and when schedules were imposed on creative personnel who then had to work within spaces or time-slots already pre-determined, are long since over.

FOR FURTHER FEADING

Spending Advertising Money (S. Broadbent, Business Publications Ltd.).
Selection of Advertising Media (J. Hobson, Business Books Ltd. for I.P.A.).
Television Advertising (D. Ingman, Business Publications Ltd.).
Handbook for Media Representatives (M. Davis, Business Publications Ltd.).
[1]*British Rate and Data* (latest issue) (Maclean-Hunter Ltd.).
Media Planning (J. Adams, Business Books Ltd. for I.P.A.).

[1] This contains advertisement rates for all media and is published regularly.

CHAPTER NINE

Sales Promotion

ADVANTAGES AND LIMITATIONS OF SALES PROMOTION

WE begin by clarifying the terms used in this area of marketing operations. Sometimes sales promotion is called *merchandising*. It is also called *below the line*[1] activity. All these terms mean the same thing, namely activity designed to obtain a physical response, i.e., a direct spur to action.

Sales promotion is not new. The need for this *link* between advertising and point of sale was recognised long ago, and promotions were a common feature even before the end of the last century. In recent years, however, their use has mushroomed in response to growing competition. The multiplicity of products and services now available to the consumer in all fields frequently creates the need to provide an *additional incentive* for the purchase of a particular brand, over and above the proposition itself. Promotions (money-off offers, free gifts, competitions, etc.) can be an important factor in getting the consumer to:

(i) try a new product
(ii) use an existing product for the first time
(iii) use more of a given product

So far as its influence on the retailer is concerned, it can:

(i) help to induce initial stocking
(ii) stimulate heavier stocking
(iii) encourage increased product display.

Its advantages are so immediate and obvious, not least in that sales results can often be measured accurately in relation to expenditure (unlike advertising), that it is not surprising that sales promotion is a popular

[1] Conversely, media advertising is sometimes referred to as *above the line* activity. This distinction, which has the merit of eliminating ambiguity, derives from Proctor & Gamble Ltd.

marketing tool. So much so, in fact, that in recent years there has been a shift in total expenditure from media advertising to sales promotion; indeed some marketing men have even forecast a major decline in the former. However, this is unlikely. Promotions are essentially a short-term device, as one of the world's leading research companies (A. C. Nielsen) has demonstrated many times. Its studies over the years reveal:

(i) That most promotions give only a temporary boost to sales and that, for long-term stability, media advertising is still an essential ingredient in the majority of consumer markets.

(ii) That promotions rarely create an exclusive identity or 'image' for a product in the way that media advertising can, thus their influence on brand loyalty is limited.

Therefore, it is unwise to regard promotions as a substitute for media advertising. They are *complementary*. Both activities have a part to play. Each one can do things which the other cannot, and the best marketing plan is one which achieves the right balance between advertising and promotion for a given project.

This will vary in accordance with products and even more particularly with markets. For example, promotions usually have greater *relative* importance in high-volume, high-purchasing-frequency markets, where product differentiation tends to be marginal. Thus in grocery markets, where products in many categories pose problems of choice, promotions are a major feature (in some categories, promotion expenditure is equal to the money spent on media advertising). However, in—say—clothing markets, where purchasing is relatively infrequent for major items, promotions have less significance and are thus less frequently employed.

OBJECTIVES OF PROMOTIONS

As with any other activity, it is important to set objectives for a promotion. It is not enough to make vague statements such as 'they will give the saleman a talking point with the trade' or 'they will create interest at point of sale'. Of course, they should do these things, but they are a means to an end and not an adequate reason in themselves for mounting a promotion. Thus objectives should, as always, be precise and whenever possible capable of measurement.

One of the major purposes of promotions is, of course, to increase sales of a given product. And since the medium is so flexible this objective can be refined in order to pin-point a particular product size, e.g., if the sales of a large size need boosting, an incentive can be devised to induce consumers to buy it (switching the consumer from smaller sizes to larger sizes is known as *trading up*). Similarly, the manufacturer might want the consumer to buy a different variety in the same range, e.g., grapefruit squash instead of lemon squash; again the promotion can be directed to this particular objective.

The two examples given highlight the strategic use of sales promotion rather than its merely tactical use. To 'trade up' consumers means that more of the product is bought and this encourages heavier consumption, bearing in mind also that the profit yield on larger-sizes is frequently greater for the manufacturer both absolutely and in percentage terms. It also potentially puts the consumer out of the market for a competitive product for a longer period. Similarly, to switch consumers from one flavour to another can help immediate inventory problems but can also be a factor in ensuring that the consumer's desire for variety is met by that manufacturer rather than by a competitor.

It will be seen, therefore, that in planning promotions reference should be made to the deeper issues involved and not merely to shifting so many units in such and such a time. In other words, promotions should be used to help solve marketing problems no less than immediate sales problems.

Problems and Opportunities

Promotions are flexible, but by their very nature they are not selective. For instance, the purpose of a money-off offer is primarily to induce people to try the product for the first time and, all things being equal, it is frequently successful in achieving this aim. However, existing users will also get the benefit of this subsidy, when they would have bought the product anyway. This is inevitable (and indeed may have residual benefits in terms of creating goodwill among existing users), but it has to be accepted rather than aimed for.

Timing is important. If a promotion is based on a competition where holidays are the prizes, it is useless to mount this when the majority of people have already decided their vacation plans. Thus such an incentive should be arranged to co-incide with the period of the year when holidays are under consideration, namely January-March. Another aspect of timing is *duration*. The trade and the consumer will quickly get tired of most promotions if they drag on. Thus 4–8 weeks is the optimum time, although, where trading stamps are concerned, the nature of such a device is, of course, quite different. Even here, however, changes of tempo may be desirable, e.g., double or even treble stamp deals for given periods.

The attitude of the trade can make or mar a promotion and it is important to bear in mind that retailers often have a different interest or at least a different approach to that of a manufacturer. Many do not like free samples offered by the latter. While these may have an important bearing on future sales, retailers feel they should be selling them not having them given away. Similarly, they do not like coupons or vouchers since these cause administrative problems. Therefore, consumer promotions have to be 'sold' to the trade not less than to the consumer and are frequently linked with special bonuses to retailers to ensure co-operation at the all important point of sale.

Trade promotions are desirable and indeed common. These are usually linked with sales; for example, retailers can be provided with the opportunity of entering a trade competition with the number of entries contingent upon the size of order placed. Alternatively, a trade promotion can be hooked on to a consumer promotion. If the latter is concerned with the offer of articles (premiums) at a specially reduced price plus product labels, the retailer can be provided with a choice of the same articles *free*, provided he places an order of a given size and guarantees that he will support the consumer promotion in terms of appropriate product

Get your
own Special
Homepride
Flour Grader
only
3/6
with 2
special
Homepride
coupons
Homepride
SELF-RAISING FLOUR

How to adopt a lovable, hard-working Homepride Flour Grader

1. Go to your shop. **2.** Look for the special 3 lb. bags of Homepride – self-raising or plain – announcing our flour-shaker offer. **3.** Collect the coupons from 2 bags. **4.** Send them with a P.O./cheque for 3/6. And he's all yours.

The best looking flour-shaker you ever saw. 9" tall in unbreakable plastic. Easy to refill. And very versatile. Take off his hat – and he'll shake or pour. Put it back on – and he's an airtight store . . . keeps flour or other foods clean and dry.

So you see: our Flour Grader flour shaker's not just a pretty face. Mind you, if it's the only way he can get you to adopt him, he's quite prepared just to stand there and look lovable.

This is an example of how an advertising theme can be carried over into the sales promotion area. Here is a premium offer for a flour container based on the cartoon character 'Fred' who explains the product benefits in Homepride TV commercials. Note also that it is directly relevant to the product; a classic case of using a premium not merely as a short-term sales-building device but one which will provide a continuous in-home reminder of Homepride for many years (Reproduced by courtesy of Spillers Ltd. Agency: Geers Gross Advertising Ltd.)

display. In trade promotions, a distinction is frequently made between the store *proprietor,* who will derive the benefit from special terms or incentives, and the *sales staff* who do not. Therefore, provision is also made for the latter to be given special incentives for stimulating individual product sales, although, of course, the agreement of the owner is essential and is not always easy to get, since he is concerned with selling *all* his products and not merely those of the manufacturer concerned.

DIFFERENT TYPES OF PROMOTIONS

Sampling

This means providing a free sample of a product, often but not always a new product, in the hope that people will use it, and having used it will be satisfied enough to buy it in future. This is an effective device to get people to *try*, although naturally it is expensive. It can be done nationally or regionally and through a variety of means:

Door-to-door sampling. One of the most common is door-to-door distribution. Care has to be exercised in ensuring that the product can be put through the letter box (if the householder is out). Obviously anything large, breakable or potentially dangerous, such as a razor blade, is not feasible. There are companies specialising in door-to-door distribution which is frequently carried out by casual or part-time labour under the supervision of trained permanent staff.

Sampling by post. This is another method of distributing free samples, although it is more expensive. It has the advantage of being more 'authoritative' in that it has gone through the mails rather than being found on the doormat. Detergent and toothpaste manufacturers have employed this method on a number of occasions.

Sampling from magazines. This is when the product is attached to or included between the covers of a magazine. Very suitable for a compact product such as a shampoo sachet. This has the advantage of being a joint promotion, of benefit to the manufacturer and the publishers of the magazine. It is seldom used for new products, since magazine publishers are usually unwilling to take a chance with a new product which may not be successful.

Exhibitions and in-store sampling. Samples can be given away at such exhibitions as 'Ideal Home' and also in department and other stores. Food and drink items are particularly suitable for such operations since they can be tasted on the spot, with provision made for follow-up purchase.

Banded packs. A product can be banded free of charge to an existing product (e.g., a tablet of soap to a tube of toothpaste). Two things are important here. First, the existing product has to be a fast seller in order that the sample can be widely and swiftly distributed. Secondly, the two products must be generally *related.* To band a toilet soap to a household detergent product could create the wrong connection in the consumer's mind.

Distribution to special audiences. Some commercial companies provide a special service whereby they obtain and distribute, on behalf of manufacturers, samples of appropriate products to mothers with newly born babies in hospitals and maternity homes. This idea has been extended to cover other groups who are easily pin-pointed, i.e., hotel guests, school leavers, etc.

Couponing. A variant of the physical sample, whereby a coupon is provided which either entitles the recipient to a sample of the product free or at a reduced, introductory offer. Coupons may be distributed door-to-door, through the post or incorporated in press or magazine advertisements. The magazine 'Shopping' specialises in manufacturers' offers, including the provision of coupons which can be detached. It is distributed free and is a popular vehicle which reaches a total of about 13 million households.

Premiums

An article offered free or at a reduced price which is contingent upon the purchase of a branded product is called a *premium*. Premiums divide into two:

Free premiums
Self-liquidating Premiums

Free premiums. These are articles banded to existing products and given away free as an inducement to purchase. The most frequent use of free premiums is in connection with fast moving, repeat purchase products such as toothpaste, toilet soap and packaged grocery lines (they are also used by magazine publishers as a circulation-building device). By their very nature, free premiums in this context are low priced items: plastic spoons, rainhats, paper transfers, etc. Clearly it would be a waste of time to expect consumers to send in for these gifts, which is why they are always distributed with the 'parent' product.

In the consumer durable field, however, entirely different types of free premiums are used. Such articles, ranging from toasters to electric fires, are offered with the purchase of major items of equipment—refrigerators, storage heaters, gas cookers, etc. These offers are made as alternatives to the cash allowance *trade-in,* and frequently work better in that a cash incentive may hardly be noticed where a major purchase is concerned, whereas free premiums of the type mentioned constitute tangible and desirable pieces of equipment.

Self-liquidating premiums. These are articles which are offered to the consumer at a reduced price, plus one, two or more labels of the promoted product. The term self-liquidating means self-financing. In other words, the manufacturer buys the items at a keen price and ensures that all his handling costs are built into the price at which the article is offered to the consumer. This price must still, of course, be lower than the consumer would normally buy it at and it must represent a genuine, good-value bargain, bearing in mind that the manufacturer's reputation and that of his brand are at stake. The result is something which benefits the manufacturer and the consumer. Many premium offers are tested regionally, to gauge consumer acceptance, before such promotions are launched nationally. This is to establish which of a number of premium items are likely to be most successful rather than as a hedge against purchasing of premium supplies. The latter are rarely bought *en bloc* by the manufacturer but are usually obtained from a *Premium Supply Company*. The latter undertakes to provide a wide range of suitable products from stock, mostly standard items such as rugs, cutlery, clocks. etc. as required, obviating the necessity for the manufacturer to make any large-scale commitment.

Price Promotions

These, as the term implies, are promotions based on price incentives. The classic example is the straight price cut offered by the manufacturer or retailer. This will vary with the price level of the product in question, 2p off a tube of shaving cream or jar of instant coffee is reasonable but would, of course, be ludicrous for an electric razor.

A variation of this is a price reduction geared to the *next purchase* of a given product. The vehicle is usually the label itself (specially printed) or a voucher. The initial purchase is bought at full price (although a price cut can operate even at the first stage); then, by subsequent presentation of the label or voucher to the retailer, the consumer can get a reduction for the next purchase. The manufacturer can ring the changes here by making the reduction effective for *another product* from his range.

Price promotions can also be used in terms of *special bargain* packs, e.g., three tablets of soap for the price of two. These work successfully if the product is likely to be used fairly frequently but not otherwise.

Actual money can be and has been used in this area, namely the banding of coins on to tubes of toothpaste and other toiletry articles. This has considerable novelty value although, of course, there is a security hazard where retail sales staff and, indeed, shoppers are concerned.

One important point should be made vis-a-vis manufacturers' price promotions. These cannot be made at the retailers' expense and normal trade margins apply, no matter how extensive the price incentive offered to the consumer (unless there is joint agreement to cut prices).

Competitions

These are a frequently used promotion device, the chief requirements being an exciting prize structure (cash equivalents are always provided and nearly always taken by the winner/s; however, it is still necessary to offer exotic prizes to add interest to and sometimes a focal point for the competition). Many competitions are built round the product itself, readers being asked to put product advantages in order and then to devise a slogan. These are called '*grid*' *competitions* and they have the advantage that the product's selling points are closely scrutinised by those who enter and indeed by many others. The number of entries for the majority of competitions is contingent upon the number of product labels or carton tops sent in.

Personality Promotions

These are promotions which require extensive advertising, wherein consumers are offered cash prizes if they have supplies of a product or products when visited at their houses. Such promotions are popular with the public and are usually effective, but they are very expensive to organise, both in terms of providing 'personality' teams and extensive prize money, and can be employed only by major manufacturers or producers. To keep faith with the public it is essential for every part of the country to be visited (if, as is usual, such a promotion is nationwide) and it goes without saying that a lot of people must be called on and given the opportunity to win a prize.

Trading Stamps

These are now an established and widely used promotional device, employed mostly by retailers in the grocery and garage trades. Despite criticism of trading stamps, they have proved their value both as sales *and* franchise builders for retailers who use them, since they are popular with a large section of the population for whom they satisfy the 'collecting' instinct which most of us have. By far the most widely collected stamps in Britain are GREEN SHIELD.

Displays

In the retail selling situation, display is all important and a considerable proportion of total promotional funds is expended on the provision of showcards, window stickers and all manner of devices which feature a reminder of, and selling points for, a wide variety of products. In recent years, promotion philosophy has hardened in favour of linking displays with actual products, hence the growing use of self-selection display units which embody products *and* display material combined. The pressure on the retailers' available space is such that a manufacturer's in-store display space has to be virtually (and sometimes actually) rented, hence the necessity for achieving maximum selling opportunity and selling stimulus in which the product itself is made to play a crucial part.

Exhibitions

In some fields, particularly in industrial, pharmaceutical and engineering markets, exhibitions are such a vital part of total marketing that it is, perhaps, invidious to mention such activity merely in passing. Even in consumer fields they can make a significant contribution to marketing operations, as is demonstrated by the 'Ideal Home' and 'Motor Show' exhibitions held annually. Their value lies in the fact that they combine in themselves a whole range of marketing and selling activity; they provide information about products, both through personal contact and through literature, demonstrate products, provide the opportunity whereby these products can be tried by the prospective buyer and, finally, they can be and are a vehicle for actually selling products.

FOR FURTHER READING

This subject is covered in the books on Marketing listed in Chapter 2. Three further books you will find helpful are:

Marketing for the Developing Company (J. Winkler, Hutchinson Publishing Group Ltd.).
The Practice of Marketing (D. W. Smallbone, Staples Press Ltd.).
Sales Promotion Handbook (G. C. Aspley, Dartnell Corporation.).
Guide to Sales Promotion (I.P.A. publication).

CHAPTER TEN

Media Research and Advertisement Testing

In Chapter 3, we discussed the use of research as an aid to marketing judgement. Here we examine the ways in which it is employed to help improve *advertising efficiency*. Research in advertising[1] divides into two:

(i) Its use in determining the size and composition of media audiences; this is known as MEDIA RESEARCH.

(ii) Its use in assessing the efficiency of the advertising message; this is known as ADVERTISEMENT TESTING.

MEDIA RESEARCH

Press

The circulation-assessment of the majority of publications is done by the AUDIT BUREAU OF CIRCULATIONS, a body which provides an independent calculation for its members of the number of copies sold of each publication. Where publications are not in membership, they provide an *estimate* of their paid-for circulation, often based on a similar form of auditing technique. Therefore, except for a few fringe publications whose circulation figures are suspect, the advertiser can generally have confidence in the reliability of circulation data. Such information is essential. Advertisement rates are based on circulation and the advertiser must have accurate information about how many people he can reach in relation to what he has to pay (and whether it is worth it). Circulation-auditing records the number of copies sold; however, while publications are brought by the individual they are read by others also (in the case of magazines, there is often considerable 'passing-on'). Thus circulation does not take into account total *readership* or *who* reads (i.e., readership

[1] Evaluation of competitive advertising expenditure (see Chapter 3) is, of course, important.

profile). To obtain such data it is necessary to conduct *readership surveys*.

Since the 1930s such surveys have been a constant feature of the advertising scene. They are based on the market research principles and techniques outlined in Chapter 3, namely samples of the population are interviewed at regular intervals and questioned about the newspapers and magazines they read (special questionnaire-skills are employed to minimise 'prestige' answers, e.g., too many people claiming to read 'The Times'). On this basis it is possible to define both the total readership and the readership profile for each major publication[1] and thus to direct the advertising message more accurately and economically. The scope and cost of these surveys necessitates collective organization and financing by the advertising industry, and the operation is centrally controlled by a body called JICNARS (Joint Industry Committee for National Readership Surveys). Needless to say all information is released, whether or no it is favourable to an individual publication. Readership data from this source is supplemented by surveys carried out among media owners themselves. Such surveys are usually conducted by leading research companies and the information therefore is reliable and is valued by advertisers and agencies.

Commercial Television

Information about the total number of television sets in use is readily available but, of course, not everyone is looking at TV the whole time. Moreover, a good percentage of those who do view watch B.B.C. as well as I.T.V. Therefore, the problem of identifying the number of viewers on the commercial channel who are potentially available to the advertiser is much more complex than that of identifying press readership. It is solved by a device called the SET-meter which is attached to the TV receivers of a *sample* of the population. This records what B.B.C. and I.T.V. programmes are seen by the sample, which is structured so that it is representative of all viewers. Each programme is given a rating in accordance with the number of people who watch it (e.g., a rating of 30 means that 30% of the total audience see it) and thus the advertiser can deter-

[1] Clearly it is only possible to cover widely read press media.

mine precisely what he gets for his money. While this is post hoc information, he can, of course, broadly predict in advance what audience he is likely to get at any time by reference to current rating data, bearing in mind that it provides a minute-by-minute-check of who is looking in and who is not. The patterns of viewing which have emerged from continuous use of the SET-meter device and the notebooks filled in regularly by the viewing household (the samples are changed periodically to prevent the development of conditioned or atypical viewing habits) enable the TV contractors to structure their rates accordingly. Broadly, there is *peak-viewing* time (7.00–10.00 p.m.) and *off-peak* time (time outside this spectrum).

Again the provision of television audience data is organised and financed by the advertising industry, the controlling body in this case being JICTAR (Joint Industry Committee for Television Advertising Research) which publishes weekly reports.

All other Media

The responsibility for the provision of media research data rests with the owners themselves. Surveys are carried out by them from time to time which estimate audiences for outdoor and cinema media, and for Radio Luxembourg. These are based on the research principles which apply to the press readership surveys and are generally regarded as being reliable (with direct mail the audience is already defined and quantified and the problem for the direct mail company, therefore, is to ensure that its mailing lists are accurate and up to date).

ADVERTISEMENT TESTING

From Chapter 6 you will have seen that advertising is only one of several influences on sales. At this stage of development, it is not possible, in most cases, to isolate the relative effectiveness of each influence. All that can be tested with an advertisement or campaign, therefore, are its *communication* and *memorability* factors, i.e.:

Comprehension

Is the advertising message understood?

Belief

Does the viewer/reader accept what is being said?

Impact

What can the viewer/reader remember of what he has seen or read?

Attitude

Has it changed the consumer's attitude towards the product (for better or worse)?

Overall Reaction

Is there something the consumer particularly likes or dislikes about any element of the advertising message?

Testing involves the basic market research technique of selecting broadly representative samples of consumers, although there are a number of different *methods* of eliciting response.

PRE-TESTING

As the word implies these are tests carried out *before* the advertising is due to appear. Whatever the method used, all pre-testing suffers from the unreal conditions under which it takes place and its divorcement from the sales situation. However, it can be extremely useful in pin-pointing any obvious deficiencies in communication.

Television

(i) *Group discussions.* The TV commercial is exposed to a group of respondents, followed by subsequent discussion on reactions to it. This is a quick, fairly inexpensive way of finding out any major communication negatives. Because of the nature of the technique (i.e., unstructured interviewing), points that arise, either favourable or unfavourable, can be explored in depth. The disadvantage is that this method is feasible only with small numbers of people.

(ii) *Theatre testing.* One widely used method embodies the exposure of TV commercials to respondents in a theatre. The sample varies from between 100–300 people and is recruited by post or personal interview. 'Commercial' testing sessions (which include the screening of entertainment films as well as commercials in order to provide a 'normal' framework of viewing) are run by experienced comperes who call out the different questions to be answered. Distributed questionnaires are then self-completed by the audience.

The kinds of questions asked relate to brand recall, the advertising message communicated, any particular likes or dislikes about the commercial, believability about its claims, the likelihood of purchase, etc. The results achieved are given 'scores' and these can be compared with scores for previous commercials tested by this method in the same product field.

(iii) *Coach method.* This is an alternative to theatre testing, the commercial being exposed to respondents (usually about 6 at a time) in a coach. It has the advantage of mobility since a coach can be taken anywhere, whereas theatre testing must be done in urban centres. Moreover, sample recruitment is easier.

Press

(i) *Group discussions.* These can be used for testing a press advertisement or campaign as well as a TV commercial.

(ii) *Folder test.* A folder of advertisements is made up which contains the advertisement under test, together with 4 or 5 other (control) advertisements. Respondents are not initially given any indication which advertisement the interviewer is concerned with. They are asked to look through the folder which is then removed. Questions are then put to them about *all* the advertisements (e.g., name of brands advertised, which stands out, etc.). Only when a general benchmark has been established does the interviewer then focus on the advertisement under test, checking the communication factors referred to earlier.

A sample of between 100 and 200 respondents is normally used, interviewing taking place in the street or in the home of the respondent.

This method can also be used to compare two alternative advertisements for a product. Two *matched samples* (each of 100–200, both samples with the same characteristics) are selected. One advertisement (plus control advertisements) is exposed to one sample and the alternative advertisement (with the same control advertisements) to the other. Results are then compared.

(iii) *Dummy magazine.* A dummy magazine is made up containing the ad under test, together with other advertisements, plus editorial matter. Respondents are then handed copies and asked to consider what they think of the dummy magazine in terms of its total content. Later, respondents are called on and questioned about the advertisement under test to see how well it has been noticed, what has been remembered, etc. This method has the advantage of removing a great deal of the artificiality of pre-testing, although it tends to be expensive and, of course, requires a considerable amount of organising.

POST-TESTING

This involves testing an advertisement *after* it has actually appeared on the screen or in print. It is carried out under more realistic conditions than pre-testing. However, it cannot, of course, help in the development of the creative approach; moreover, it takes place when a certain commitment (and investment) has already been made. Checks on specific details of communication are also difficult because of the inevitable time lapse between advertisement exposure and the interview.

Television

24-hour recall. This is a widely used method of post-testing. The day following the appearance of a TV commercial, a sample of respondents who were viewing at that time are interviewed in their homes to find out if they spontaneously recall the commercial and, if they do, what they can remember about it. This is a good way to measure impact (although, of course, there is no proven correlation between recall and sales effectiveness) but less satisfactory for checking other factors of communication since people can rarely play back in great detail what they see or hear in advertisements.

Press

(i) *Gallup field readership index.* This is a continuous study being carried out where readers of newspapers and magazines are concerned. Readers of a specific publication are interviewed about their reading behaviour in regard to a particular issue. They are taken right through the publication and asked in relation to each page which particular features, if any, they remember having seen and read (including advertisements as well as editorial matter). The advertisement is given a 'score' for the degree of recall (what was seen and read) which it achieves, and average scores are built up over a time for different advertisements in terms of their general layout, their positions and the publications in which they appear. This is a valuable method of post-testing because it embraces evaluation of the context in which an advertisement appears as well as the advertisement itself.

(ii) *Split-run test.* This method is used to test the relative communication efficacy of two alternative advertisements in a totally realistic situation. Arrangements are made with a leading national newspaper or magazine to run both advertisements in the same issue, but to split them evenly[1] during the printing so that, when the publication is distributed, one half of the readership is exposed to one advertisement and the other half to the alternative. A common procedure is to make a 'hidden offer' in each advertisement, usually for a free booklet. No prominence is given to this offer, and for readers of the publication to learn that it is being made they must read the advertisements all the way through. Applications for booklets from each advertisement are assessed (they are keyed for response-identification, e.g., Dept. A and B respectively). The one which pulls the bigger response is judged to have the capacity to attract higher readership; while this does not prove that such readership leads to higher sales, it is a prima facie indication of greater communication effectiveness.

[1] or by regions

PRE- AND POST-TESTING COMBINED

A campaign can be tested combining the two methods. Prior to the start of the campaign, a sample of consumers can be interviewed and their attitudes to and awareness of the brand to be advertised can be measured. At the end of the campaign, an identical operation can be mounted using a 'matched' sample. In this way, the effect of the campaign can be assessed in terms of its influence, for good or bad, in changing attitudes and awareness.

FOR FURTHER READING

Measuring Advertising Readership and Results (D. Starch, McGraw-Hill Publishing Co. Ltd.).
Testing Advertisements: A Study of Copy Testing (L. E. Firth, McGraw-Hill Publishing Co. Ltd.).
Attention and Interest Factors in Advertising (H. J. Rudolph, Funk & Wagnalls).
Producing Useful Media Research (I.P.A. booklet).
Review of Media and Product Research Sources (I.P.A. publication).

CHAPTER ELEVEN

Controls in Advertising

LEGAL CONTROLS ON ADVERTISING

IMPRESSIONS die hard, especially when they are derived from a vivid past. For example, it is often said that the people of Soviet Russia form their view of British life from the novels of Charles Dickens. Although he has been dead for 100 years, his work is still felt to be an accurate description of conditions in this country today.

Advertising suffers from the same mythology. Few people can fail to have been exposed to examples of the advertising horrors of the nineteenth century: the extravagant claims made for quack remedies, the unscrupulous use of past Royal personages to 'sponsor' advertised brands, the shameless appeals to fear and human gullibility. All this, of course, is as dead as a doornail and has been for many years. But advertising has never entirely shaken off the 'image' which was created for it in those far off days and there are critics even now who seem to believe that advertisers have unbridled licence.

This is very far from the truth. For one thing there are some 60 Statutes and Statutory Instruments which, in one way or another, affect advertising. One of the most important of these is the TRADE DESCRIPTIONS ACT 1968, which is designed to protect the trade and public not only from false advertising claims but indeed from false claims in all areas of marketing activity, on labelling and packaging right through to price tickets in the shop. Its provisions cover the spoken word as well as the written word and breaches of them can lead to severe penalties not only for offending firms and companies but also for *individuals* in them. The scope of this Act (and indeed of other legislation which affects marketing and advertising) is far too wide to deal with adequately in this book. Briefly, however, it places the onus on manufacturers and retailers to avoid false descriptions made on behalf of the goods and services they offer.

CASE FOR A VOLUNTARY CONTROL SYSTEM

There is also a strong and effective control system which the industry has imposed on itself to prevent abuses in advertising. The first question that arises is: why maintain a voluntary system when so much legislation exists? The answer is that legislation is concerned with black and white issues. It has to be tightly drawn and thus it can never be as flexible or as sensitive to change in controlling advertising as the voluntary system. Nor can it cover the range of restraints which the latter system imposes, e.g., in matters of taste, comparison, etc. This was recognised by the Government and by the Civil Service when the Trade Descriptions Act was passed in 1968. The official view was that while certain aspects of the problem should be dealt with by legislation there was a wide range of potential problems remaining which could be tackled by the industry itself. This view is still held and what it amounts to is firm recognition of the effectiveness of a voluntary[1] control system, which is regarded as *complementary* to legislation.

THE STRUCTURE OF THE SYSTEM

The success of the whole operation rests upon its structure. In a sentence, it is a tripartite two-tier system. Tripartite—i.e., the three parts of the advertising industry: advertisers, advertising agencies and media, all media. Two-tier—i.e., an independent body at the top and an all-industry committee beneath it. These two tiers are the Advertising Standards Authority (A.S.A.) and the Code of Advertising Practice Committee (C.A.P.). The whole structure is underpinned and paid for by the Advertising Association. The British public pays not a penny.

[1] Voluntary means that the industry has voluntarily imposed this system of control upon itself; it does not mean that advertisers are free to disregard the regulations of the system.

ADVERTISING STANDARDS AUTHORITY (A.S.A.),
1 BELL YARD, FLEET STREET, LONDON, W.C.2

This is the ultimate authority in the control system. The A.S.A. was established by the industry in 1962 with the object of: 'the promotion and enforcement through the United Kingdom of the highest standards of advertising in all media so as to ensure in co-operation with all concerned that no advertising contravenes or offends against these standards, having regard *inter alia* to the British Code of Advertising Practice'. It consists of eleven members, including the Chairman. The Chairman and five of the members (i.e., the majority) are *not* engaged in advertising, while the remaining five are. All serve as *individuals* and not as representatives of any trade, profession, organisation or company.

The A.S.A., although financed by the advertising industry through the Advertising Association, is entirely *independent*. It is not biased in favour of the manufacturer or the consumer or any other section of the community. Its task is to act as a watchdog on advertising and it fulfils this task with an energy and impartiality which commands respect from all quarters. The A.S.A. maintains close liaison with the C.A.P. Committee (and indeed all other sections of the control system) and it can and does intervene on its own account to call for amendments and improvements to the Code if it thinks fit.

In addition to its basic function of overseeing the control system, the A.S.A. is also an important channel through which representations and complaints about advertising are directed. Anyone, private individuals as well as those representing corporate bodies, has the right to approach the A.S.A., who ensures that all matters brought to its attention are rigorously investigated. From time to time, the A.S.A. issues guidance to advertisers and agencies which covers not only advertising practice but also advice on the ways in which sales promotion programmes should be conducted.

CODE OF ADVERTISING PRACTICE COMMITTEE (C.A.P.)

The Committee consists of representatives of 18 advertising organisations representing advertisers, agencies and all media. The television companies are represented by their association (Independent Television Companies Association) even although the medium of television is controlled by a public body (Independent Broadcasting Authority). Each association may be represented by one permanent official and one member, who may have a named alternate for meetings. In practice, one Association (Periodical Publishers Association) has two members, one representing general magazines and another trade and technical magazines; and the five poster organizations are represented by one person.

The Chairman is elected for a period of two years and is invariably an advertiser. The Vice-Chairman is Chairman of the Copy Advisory Panel, a small group of members of the Committee which deals with copy problems. None of the members of the Committee is paid a fee.

The Committee meets once a month. The C.A.P. Officials also meet separately once a month to deal with points of detail and arrange the agenda for the C.A.P. Committee.

The Chairman of A.S.A. attends, by invitation, meetings of the C.A.P. Committee.

How the Code is Administered

The Code is administered by the C.A.P. Committee. Its task is to keep the Code under constant review, to make whatever changes are necessary to strengthen it in the light of changing circumstances and to ensure that its decisions are communicated to the industry at large.

The Code is implemented by all who work in advertising; thus *advertisers* and *agencies* have to ensure that advertisements they offer for publication conform to its requirements. Similarly *media owners* ensure that all advertisements received for publication or transmission are checked and that there is no breach of the Code.

Media owners have a vital role to play in making certain that the Code is observed—not only have they established individual vetting machinery for each medium but also collective machinery to ensure common standards of evaluation and action. It has long been a practice for media organisations to have their own copy (checking) committee whose task it is to decide upon the acceptability of copy of the particular medium involved. Television is a different case, being partly statutory. The non-statutory part, the Copy Clearance Department of the Independent Television Companies Association, vets every single script and film before transmission and is a complete operation. (As this book goes to press, arrangements are being finalised to ensure that parallel procedures are established for commercial radio, which is expected to be in operation by late 1973/early 1974.)[1]

The outdoor advertising bodies have had a censorship Committee since 1890. It is formed on an *ad hoc* basis, consisting of three or four people gathered together to adjudicate on any particular poster which may seem questionable. If the decision is not favourable the poster does not appear.

The national and provincial press combine in forming a Joint Copy Committee, and the Periodical Publishers Association has its own committee dealing with general, trade and technical magazines.

All this machinery helps to ensure that if an advertisement offends the Code—bearing in mind that the body ultimately responsible for interpretation of the Code is the C.A.P. Committee—it will not be published in any medium. Indeed, a company's entire advertising can be ruled unacceptable and refused by all media. Thus, a powerful *sanction* against misleading advertising is available and, indeed, has been applied on a number of occasions. It could well be argued that this sanction is a more effective deterrent than impersonal fines payable upon breaches of the law and *it is the bedrock of the voluntary control system.* One thing should be noted: the purpose of vetting advertisements is to *prevent* abuses, although should they still arise the control machinery can and does take action to prevent a recurrence. This underlines the point that, in addition

[1] In statutory terms both Commercial Television and Commercial Radio will be controlled by a newly established joint body called the *Independent Broadcasting Authority*.

to prevention, the control system embraces two other activities: *monitoring* and *investigation.*

The ultimate responsibility for ensuring that these activities are carried out is, of course, the A.S.A. However, its executive arm is the C.A.P. Committee. The monitoring side of C.A.P.'s job involves close and continuous scrutiny of a wide range of publications to make certain that the Code is being observed. These include 'fringe' publications, where breaches of the Code are more likely to occur, as well as major publications. When it is established that the Code has been breached, it approaches the offender direct and advises the publisher. The result of C.A.P. intervention is the withdrawal or amendment of the offending advertisement.

Finally, the C.A.P. Committee investigates actual complaints about advertisements. These may arise from members of the public or from other advertisers. In some instances C.A.P. will be conducting investigations on behalf of the A.S.A., bearing in mind that the A.S.A. is the principal body through which complaints are channelled—but C.A.P. can and does act on its own initiative if it thinks necessary. If a complaint is upheld (a great many complaints are, of course, found on investigation to be groundless) the necessary action is taken to prevent a recurrence.

General Comments

It must not be imagined that the existence of a comprehensive control system implies a battery of unscrupulous advertisers straining at the leash to mislead the public. Reputable advertisers, who are in the majority, know that this is not in their long-term interests. The public may be persuaded to buy a product once, on the basis of extravagant or misleading claims, but if it fails to live up to the promise it will not be bought again. It should be remembered that advertising clearly *identifies* a brand, thus it can become a two-edged weapon if it is misused and most advertisers are enlightened enough to recognise this. They also recognise that misleading advertising brings all advertising into disrepute, so the short-term gains it brings are quickly cancelled out.

In point of fact, the most misleading advertising is perpetrated by the

THE CODE OF ADVERTISING PRACTICE

The general Code has 20 rules in all, which embody both the positive and the negative. ***Positively*,** there is a firm requirement that all *descriptions*, *claims* and *comparisons* must be capable of substantiation without delay.

In regard to the ***negative*,** the Code specifically forbids the following:

the use of any description, claim or comparison, directly or by implication, which is misleading about the product advertised or about any other product;

any indication that the product advertised, or any ingredient, has some special quality or property which cannot be substantiated;

the denigration of other products directly or by implication;

the imitation of competitive advertising in a way that is likely to mislead or confuse;

the false or misleading use of scientific terms and statistics;

the exploitation, without justification, of fear;

the exploitation of superstition;

the use, without justifiable reason, of the description or depiction of dangerous practices or a disregard of safety;

the use in advertisiments addressed to children which might result in physical, mental or moral harm to them or which exploits their credulity;

the use of testimonials (i.e., letters from members of the public) which make claims that would not otherwise be permitted;

the execution of advertisements in a style which could be confused with editorial-matter;

the employment of inertia selling (i.e. supplying goods which have not been ordered);

misuse of the word 'free';

unsatisfactory or false guarantees.

In addition to these general prohibitions, there are special regulations covering mail order advertising, direct sale advertising, home visits by advertiser's representatives, homework schemes, instructional courses, franchise schemes, pregnancy testing and mortgage brokers.

The Code contains a special section on the advertising of *proprietary medicines*, *treatments* and *appliances*.

public itself and, while all newspapers exercise reasonable vigilance over their classified advertising columns, it will be appreciated that the control system does not and cannot operate in this area. Nor can it operate so far as the fringe 'fly-by-nighters' are concerned, except that it can prevent the pornographers and switch selling operators from advertising their wares in reputable media. Nevertheless, such people can and do use the post and shop-windows to conduct their operations, and because even such marginal activities like this can bring all advertising into disrepute, the Advertising Association is looking into this problem as this book goes to press.

These things apart, however, the voluntary control system is a powerful instrument both for protecting the public and, ultimately, for advancing the cause of advertising by helping to ensure that it is 'legal, decent, honest and truthful'.

FOR FURTHER READING

On law affecting advertising

The Law of Advertising (W. L. Leaper, Butterworth & Co. Ltd.).

Modern Advertising Law (P. Langdon-Davies, Business Books Ltd. for I.P.A.).

Advertising and the Law (F. P. Bishop, Ernest Benn Ltd.).

Advertisements in Court (John Braun, David Fanning Ltd.).

The voluntary control system

British Code of Advertising Practice

Advertising Standards Authority Annual Reports (from same address as the Code).

I.P.A. Bye-Laws (I.P.A.).

CHAPTER TWELVE

Careers in Advertising

JOBS IN ADVERTISING

It is a common experience among advertising people to be asked whether they 'draw the pictures or write the words'. This stems from fiction and films which usually highlight these parts of the business. Actually, a great many personnel do neither. As we have already seen, the advertising business is a complex one which requires administrators and specialists of all kinds as well as creative people.

In Chapter 4, the job functions in advertising were broadly covered. Let us now take a closer look at them.

ADVERTISING AGENCIES

JOBS IN ADMINISTRATION

Account Management

This is the term applied to those agency personnel who are responsible for handling clients' business within an agency.

The key administrator in this area is the SENIOR ACCOUNT EXECUTIVE (or ACCOUNT SUPERVISOR), whose task is to initiate, organise and administer advertising operations. He also has to possess sufficient all-round marketing and advertising knowledge to be able to assess the quality of output of the agency specialists and, of course, to contribute to policy decisions.

In many agencies he is assisted by an ACCOUNT EXECUTIVE, usually younger and with less experience, but who should, in due course, be able to graduate to full account control. Some agencies also employ yet a further grade of executive, the ASSISTANT ACCOUNT EXECUTIVE. Such a man will usually be very junior, possibly even a trainee, and his task is to do the fetching and carrying for his more senior colleagues, again with the prospect of moving up the ladder as he gains experience.

All executives are answerable to an ACCOUNT DIRECTOR, the person at board level who is ultimately responsible for the accounts in question. Many directors have graduated from the executive ranks and the prospects for board-promotion in agencies are very favourable for competent and progressive account handlers.

Progress Control

The role of the executive has changed in recent years. His task now has more emphasis on policy-making and less on routine duties. The internal progressing of all stages of campaign development, therefore, is frequently delegated in agencies to personnel who are called PROGRESS CONTROLLERS or TRAFFIC CONTROLLERS. They are responsible to account management for ensuring that all work is produced to the time schedules allocated. This means that, after the initial briefing by executives, the progress men liaise with the various agency departments, progress the work, and organise review meetings at all stages right up to completion. It is essentially an organising (albeit a skilled) job and some men are content to be in it for life. For others it can be a useful stepping-stone to account management, since the work involves contact with personnel in all areas and thus provides extensive knowledge of how an agency operates.

Production

(A) *Press and Print.* When an advertisement is finalised, it has to be reproduced in a number of newspapers or magazines. To ensure a uniform appearance and quality, printing plates are produced. This involves typesetting (of texts) and blockmaking (of illustrations). Once this stage is completed, the advertisement units are then stereotyped or electrotyped to the quantities required and despatched to the publications on the schedule.

All agencies employ *production personnel,* who must acquire the necessary technical knowledge to organise the mechanical reproduction of advertisements (and of leaflets, catalogues etc.).

They are under the control of a PRODUCTION MANAGER. Some production men are in production for the whole of their careers and find it a rewarding and stimulating job. Others use production as a stepping-stone to progress control and ultimately to executive positions. The experience gained in this department is frequently of great value, since all advertising personnel should be aware of the technical aspects of advertisement reproduction and indeed of printing generally.

(B) *Television, Cinema and Radio.* Just as a press advertisement idea has to be developed into a tangible unit for reproduction and replication, so does a TV or cinema film (or, in the case of radio, a recording of the commercial). Most films are made by specialist film companies but the majority of agencies employ TV producers whose task is to brief them, cast (i.e., choose the actors) and supervise the shooting, and to make sure the films are made on time. They also have to ensure that all films conform to the requirements of the Voluntary Control System and to the Television Censorship Authority (see Chapter 11). Agency TV PRODUCERS combine administrative skills with technical know-how. While they can be, and are, recruited from the film world, they can also graduate from the ranks of the TV Department, after working in *general administrative* and *clerical jobs* associated with the production of films and commercials.

SPECIALISTS

Market Research

Research executives obtain and process the information on which marketing and advertising strategy is based. At the early stages of their career, they may well operate at RESEARCH ASSISTANT level. While this can involve all-round participation in research activities the basic task is usually to conduct Desk Research. Later, the research assistant should be able to graduate to RESEARCH EXECUTIVE and thus initiate and supervise field research projects, product testing and special assignments. All personnel are under the control of a MARKET RESEARCH MANAGER, who will usually have been through all stages of the research operation either with agencies or research companies. In bigger agencies he in turn is responsible to a RESEARCH DIRECTOR, although in some cases he may report direct to the Managing Director.

Marketing

Many agencies do not employ marketing personnel, since they argue that the function of interpeting (or even helping to evolve) clients' marketing strategy is the proper function of account management. However, there are a number who do, and they will usually be among the larger agencies and also those who are closely involved in new product development with their clients. The activities of MARKETING EXECUTIVES can vary: they may interpret marketing strategy to advertising personnel, they may help clients to establish it or they may even be the dominating element in setting up the overall plan. In all areas their task is to pinpoint marketing opportunities and to provide guidance on how they can be exploited (with special reference to the part advertising can play). Some marketing executives, however, specialise in sales promotion and the job description sometimes covers personnel who are concerned with the planning of merchandising and display programmes. When an agency does have a Marketing Department it is usually under the control of a MARKETING MANAGER, who is in turn responsible to the MARKETING DIRECTOR.

Media Planning

All agencies employ MEDIA PLANNERS, whose responsibility it is to combine statistical know-how with creative flair in planning the media which carries the advertising message. The importance of media planning is reflected in the number of agencies which now have a MEDIA DIRECTOR (that is to say the activities of this department are increasingly being represented at board level). He is usually backed by a MEDIA MANAGER who is in charge of day-to-day operations. The opportunities for promotion to media management are favourable for skilled and experienced media planners.

Media Buying

The functions of *planning* and *buying* are usually kept separate, although both are usually under the control of the Media Manager. Because the emphasis in this book has been on the planning side (in order to establish basic advertising principles) it should not be thought that buying is unimportant. There is a big demand for space and time in key national media and good buying, in terms of obtaining the best spaces and time spots at the most advantageous rates, is of considerable importance. Therefore, SPACE BUYERS and TIME BUYERS, who must be skilled negotiators and hard bargainers, are vital elements in media operations. The qualities required for buying are somewhat different from those in planning, and there is comparatively little inter-change in personnel, except in smaller agencies where the functions are sometimes combined.

Voucher Checking

When clients spend money in media, they naturally require evidence that the advertisements paid for have appeared. Therefore, it is the agency's responsibility to check on all publications in which space has been booked and to provide clients with *voucher copies,* containing evidence of advertisement appearance (TV and radio stations provide transmission certificates). The VOUCHER MANAGER is usually a person who has specialised in this task and who will continue with it during his career. VOUCHER CLERKS may also come into this category, but sometimes they are hopefuls who have started in this capacity with the intention of moving up if they can prove themselves. A number of senior advertising personnel today started their careers in this relatively humble, but important job. Voucher checking usually comes within the orbit of the Media Department.

CREATIVE PERSONNEL

Creative operations are always under the direction of a CREATIVE DIRECTOR (this is usually an actual board appointment). He is responsible for the agency's creative output and must, therefore, recruit the best talent available, lead and direct it and provide it with the right environment in which to work. He must also have the ability to evaluate creative work and be able to suggest improvements and developments where necessary. Creative Directors usually graduate from copy or design and thus are experienced in evolving as well as assessing ideas, but in the top job they must also be good administrators and be able to sell successfully the ideas which the Department produces.

Agencies employ a range of COPYWRITERS/SCRIPTWRITERS[1]. A common appointment is COPY CHIEF, that is a copywriter who supervises the work of the other writers in addition to undertaking important writing tasks himself. In some big agencies where there are creative groups or units, the senior writer in each is known as COPY GROUP HEAD. His responsibilities also include supervision of other writers. Many agencies have on their pay-roll at least one TRAINEE COPYWRITER, sometimes more.

On the design or visualising side, agencies employ supervisors called ART DIRECTORS, or when the group system operates ART GROUP HEADS. These are usually experienced visualisers who have proved their capacity to lead and inspire a team of VISUALISERS. The latter will vary in age and experience and may generally be classified as Senior, Middle-Weight and Junior, all with the chance of moving up in due course. In many agencies there are also TRAINEE VISUALISERS, young men or women who have just graduated from Art School and who are gaining their first experience of advertisement designing.

Most visualisers are capable of producing some kind of finished artwork but usually this type of work is undertaken by outside studios. Some agencies, however, employ FINISHED ARTISTS and also PHOTOGRAPHERS, but here again the majority rely on outside photographic studios.

The third basic element of the Creative Department is typography. TYPOGRAPHERS choose the typefaces in which advertisements are set; their task is a creative one as well as a mechanical one of ensuring

[1] This function is usually combined.

that headlines and texts in the chosen type or types fit the spaces provided. Such personnel tend to specialise permanently in this area, but some have shown a desire to move on and it is certainly possible to graduate to visualising from typography.

In bigger agencies, specialist creative personnel are also employed chiefly in PACKAGING, DISPLAY WORK and EXHIBITION WORK.

ADVERTISERS

The key administrative jobs on this side of the business are that of ADVERTISING MANAGER or BRAND MANAGER. Both positions roughly correspond to the agency Account Executive in that they involve responsibility for initiating and administering advertising and promotion programmes. However, the spectrum of activity covered by the Advertising or Brand Manager is wider. In addition to maining close liaison with the company's advertising agency or agencies, such personnel, particularly the Brand Manager, will be in constant touch with the laboratory, the factory, the sales force, the warehouse and other areas of company operations to co-ordinate all aspects of the development and transmission of goods from drawing board to retail outlet. They are frequently supported by an ASSISTANT ADVERTISING MANAGER or ASSISTANT BRAND MANAGER. Many Advertising Managers have had agency experience, and while this is not essential it is desirable for obvious reasons. It is also of value to Brand Managers and the 'agency route' to brand management is now almost as common as the company route, although there are, of course, a number of companies who induct and train Brand Managers themselves.

Some advertisers do not employ an advertising agency. This is either because they prefer to handle their own advertising or because the nature of their operations makes it difficult for them to use an agency. In addition, there are advertisers who, while retaining an agency, also undertake some advertising tasks themselves. In these cases, such advertisers may employ creative, media and other specialists direct (alternatively, they use them on a freelance or consultancy basis). Thus, there are company advertising operations structured very much on the lines of an advertising agency, employing the types of specialist personnel to be found therein. Even so, there are fewer advertising specialists within companies as a whole; more commonly advertisers employ *specialists in packaging, exhibition, display and print,* either in design or production, or both.

MEDIA ORGANISATIONS

In Chapter 4, we discussed the key job: ADVERTISEMENT MANAGER.

Despite his title, his function is more of a selling or indeed a marketing job and, as stated previously, the term *Sales Manager* is now increasingly being used to describe his function. Since what is being sold is advertising space or time, and given that such personnel are in close touch with agency and company advertising personnel, it is obvious that extensive knowledge of advertising is required. (Nevertheless, the path to this job is currently via sales representation. SALES REPRESENTATIVES, therefore, have the opportunity of making their way up the ladder and are becoming better equipped to do so now that they are being progressively trained by media organisations to meet the more sophisticated demands of agencies and advertisers).

So far as his advertising function is concerned, he has to adjust himself to the special demands of advertising and promoting a publication, TV or radio station both to advertisers and to the public. He is not dealing with a commodity which remains fairly constant in the short-term, but with a medium which changes frequently in terms of the features, programmes, etc. it offers to the public. Thus he must live with the editorial or programme planners in order to exploit new situations as they arise, and must also be alive to the constant need to maintain and build circulation by evolving incentives in the form of competitions, premiums, supplements, free gifts, etc.

He is supported by an ASSISTANT ADVERTISEMENT MANAGER and by other EXECUTIVES. He also frequently has at his disposal his own CREATIVE PERSONNEL, both copywriters and visualisers, and it is probably true that media organisations are second only to agencies in the employment and career opportunities they offer to creative talent, although, of course, this applies only to the bigger ones.

ANCILLARY SERVICES

A brief summary about the jobs in the main areas.

Market Research Companies

In addition to employing statisticians, computer programmers and other technical specialists, such companies also employ EXECUTIVES, whose role corresponds with that of advertising agency executives. Their task is to maintain liaison with agency and advertiser personnel who make use of the services of research companies. They must, of course, be experienced in market research and be able to help and advise on all assignments. Such experience may be gained direct or via an agency research department, and market research executives can hope to graduate to RESEARCH MANAGEMENT jobs either in this type of company or with agency, advertiser or media organisations.

Public Relations Companies

Such companies also employ EXECUTIVES both at senior and junior level. Unlike executives in other spheres, who have a range of specialist resources from which to draw, the P.R. Executive tends to devise and progress proposals and ideas initiated by himself and immediate colleagues. Indeed at the more senior level the word CONSULTANT is more appropriate and such personnel are frequently partners or directors of the company in which they serve. The path to P.R. executive positions is either direct, that is by training and progressing within P.R. companies, or via journalism in which field the executive gains contacts of great value to a P.R. company. P.R. executives may progress to MANAGEMENT jobs either in this type of company, in advertiser organisations, or in advertising agencies which provide P.R. services.

Creative Services

The most common creative services are those provided by STUDIOS. These organisations produce most of the finished artwork for press advertisements, but they also undertake extensive design and finished work for packaging, sales literature, exhibitions, displays and a wide range of activity. They are concerned more with design than with copy, but some employ copywriters and all have access to copywriters in order that they can provide a complete service if required. Most of the jobs in this area are for creative personnel, particularly artists, but many studios employ SALES EXECUTIVES to service their clients (to receive briefs, transmit them and to submit the finished assignments on time).

A growing feature, however, is the type of creative service which devises advertising campaigns for advertisers and agents. These companies employ copywriters and visualisers either full time or on a free-lance basis. They are less concerned with the services which studios provide, but may well have a link-up with them for finished artwork and other studio services to progress campaigns to artwork stage and beyond.

Advertisement printing and production

There are a number of companies which specialise in typesetting, block-making and stereotyping/electrotyping of press advertisements. In addition to employing compositors, engravers, platemakers and other specialist technical staff, they also employ SALES EXECUTIVES and PROGRESS CONTROLLERS. The former maintain close contact with agencies and advertisers, while the latter are responsible for progressing work-flow internally. Such personnel have MANAGEMENT career opportunities in this field and also opportunities to break into the agency field, via production. A number of agency executives have progressed through such companies, which provide a valuable groundwork for an advertising career as well as a career in the printing industry.

GETTING INTO ADVERTISING

Selecting the Right Job-Category

From the foregoing, you will have seen that jobs in advertising break down into three broad categories. It is vitally important that you select the right area for yourself at the outset.

(i) *Administration.* This area embraces a wide spectrum of activity, ranging in an agency through all levels of account management and covering elements such as progress control, production and voucher checking. On the advertiser front it covers advertising and brand management and supporting executive roles, and in media organisations a parallel range of functions. In account, brand and advertising management the following qualities are necessary: intelligence, the capacity for leadership, the ability to handle people, a flair for understanding complex subjects and expressing them in simple terms, an orderly mind, an even temperament, a head for detail.

(ii) *Specialists in research and media planning.* Although separate functions, market research and media planning have a great deal in common in terms of the *qualities* needed by those who specialise in these tasks. Both necessitate considerable powers of analysis, the ability to understand and interpret complex statistical data, and the capacity to communicate findings and proposals intelligibly and succinctly to the non-specialist. However, neither task turns on technical know-how alone. Both the research executive and the media planner have to blend creativity and imagination with statistics in order to get the best results.

(iii) *Creative.* While creativity is an essential element in the make-up of anyone who works in advertising, this category comprises the people who specifically create the advertising message. *Copywriters* must have the ability to produce ideas, and the discipline to mould them into a form which is dynamic yet believable, original yet relevant. They must, of course, have the capacity to write well, which in advertising means making every word count. *Visualisers* and *Artists* must also be rich in ideas which are capable, when translated into design or movement, of arresting the consumer's attention, facilitating understanding and adding to the personality of the product or service being advertised.

Qualities for a Career in Advertising

If you are at or approaching school leaving age you should have some idea now which area of the business is most likely to be suitable for your own talents and aptitude. Whatever path you take, bear in mind that there are *qualities* which every advertising man or woman needs, regardless of his or her specialisation.

You must be interested in people. Advertising is about people. Those you work with. Those to whom you communicate. To succeed in it you must understand people. To understand people you must be interested in them.

You must be dynamic. Advertising is a fast moving business subject to rapid changes in line with changes in society and the market place. You must be quick to recognise new trends and new needs, and be prepared to adapt yourself to them. If necessary you must be prepared to discard cherished ideas and methods.

You must be objective. You will be involved in operations aimed at people of diverse interests and tastes. You have to be objective, to judge things not by what you like and dislike but by the standards of the people you are communicating with.

You need energy, determination. Advertising can bring high rewards. But the demands are high. You will have to be prepared to work hard, frequently under pressure. You will experience disappointments when schemes you have sweated over are rejected by management or clients, or overtaken by events. To maintain enthusiasm and quality of output you need energy and determination, and the will to succeed in highly competitive conditions.

THE FIRST STEPS

Getting into advertising is not easy. For one thing it tends to be a highly paid business (for established personnel) and thus competition for entrance is brisk. Secondly, it is regarded, on the whole rightly, as an exciting business and this again means there is no shortage of aspirants. Moreover, advertising is not a big business in terms of the *number* of people it employs (e.g., 15,600 in I.P.A. agencies, see Chapter 4). Therefore, you should have no illusions about getting an easy ride into advertising.

On the credit side, however, advertising is a fast-moving business. Promotion can be rapid and this creates a constant need for replacement in the junior ranks. So to break in is not impossible if you are determined to do so and are prepared to persevere.

You can, of course, get valuable advice from your Careers Master, or from the Public Schools Appointment Board or the University Appointments Board (depending on your own situation). The Careers Advisory Service of the Department of Employment and Productivity is also helpful, and the advertising industry itself operates a Careers Advisory Service through the Advertising Association. Therefore, do not hesitate to get in touch with these sources, all of whom are in regular contact with the business and are very willing to give constructive and helpful information.

You are also advised to write to agencies, advertisers, media organisations and indeed ancilliary service companies *direct*. This is a common procedure and one which is perfectly acceptable. Most of the firms you write to will respond courteously and you will find a surprising number who are prepared to give you advice even if they have no vacancy to offer immediately. Of course, a lot depends on the sort of letter you write. You must sell yourself confidently and positively, but do not fall into the trap of being bombastic—or long-winded. Again you will have to demonstrate that you are serious about a career in advertising and are not merely looking for glamour or easy money. It also pays to be very clear in your mind what types of assignment you are interested in. (The names and addresses of agencies, leading advertisers and media organisations can be obtained from the *Advertiser's Annual*, published by Business Publications Ltd.)

If your aim is *agency account management*, there are a number of avenues you can explore. Most of the big agencies operate *executive trainee schemes*. Successful candidates undergo a systematic induction process which involves working in each of the main agency departments before they are assigned to an account management group. Here they work under experienced supervision until they are able to accept account handling responsibilities, which they are usually ready to do, at least in a junior capacity, within 18 months. This training is supplemented by special courses, either internal or external, or both, and trainees are paid throughout. About 100 candidates are engaged each year for such schemes, although they are usually open only to graduates.

Of course, only the bigger agencies are in a position to offer such facilities. Smaller agencies do their best to accommodate trainee executives, although here the emphasis tends to be on training through experience rather than by systematic induction. A successful candidate may be assigned straight to an account group or account executive and will be operational from the word 'go'. Naturally he will have to fetch and carry and undertake routine tasks, but the experience gained is valuable and, provided it is supplemented by extra-mural study (discussed later), there is a lot to be said for this method of entry into advertising. Alternatively, candidates may be expected to join the progress control, production or voucher department and it will be up to them to prove their capacity to move up the ladder from there. Generally speaking, the better the educational qualifications you have the better the chance you have of breaking in as a trainee executive but, if you are keen to get started, do not turn down a job in any agency department. In other words, get your feet under the table at the earliest opportunity.

A third avenue is to gain selling experience (preferably in a company concerned with fast-moving consumer goods, e.g., food or drugs) before applying to an agency. Provided you are able to demonstrate that such experience has been a genuine basis for a career in advertising (and this will show by your attitude and vocabulary), you are likely to be given an encouraging reception since you will already have something to offer in terms of your understanding of the market-place.

You may, of course, wish to start with a company and here again there are a parallel range of opportunities for the newcomer. Many bigger companies run both *general* management training schemes and *marketing* management training schemes (both of which often include exposure to advertising operations). Many schemes are available only to graduates but some opportunities exist for A-level candidates. Both schemes embody training through systematic departmental induction (in marketing training schemes they frequently involve a spell as a salesman on the road) with the advantage that the candidate's particular talents are assessed comparatively quickly and thus, after 'graduation', he can be fitted in to the area of operations for which he is best suited. Even smaller companies have vacancies for trainee executives, both in marketing and advertising, and in writing to firms you are advised to spread the net fairly widely. Remember that at this stage experience in either marketing or advertising is valuable—you can transfer from one area to the other at a later stage, if necessary.

Media organisations should not be ignored either. The two leading publishing houses, International Publishing Corporation and the Thomson Group, both operate graduate training schemes, similar to those which bigger agencies and companies offer. Even if you are not qualified to join these, there may be other opportunities for aspiring executives, given the size and activities of these and other companies in the media field. As mentioned earlier, one area which is worth exploring is that of sales representative. This provides valuable experience *and* contacts (very important in the advertising business) and it is surprising how many aspirants tend to overlook or reject this avenue, which not only can lead to bigger and better things on the media front but also provides an excellent spring-board for a career with an agency or advertiser.

Entry for Specialists

The way in for those wishing to specialise is similar to those seeking a career in administration. If you want to specialise in *copywriting* you can apply direct to agencies (there are fewer opportunities for newcomers in other areas). You will need good educational qualifications, particularly in English, and you must be able to demonstrate your capacity to write well (your letters should give you some opportunity to prove it). Bear in mind, however, that writing advertisements is a specialised task. Read the available text books and study advertisements in the press, so that you can at least grasp the rudiments of what is required in order to sell yourself effectively at interviews. Do not give the impression that you are a frustrated novelist looking for a second-best career for easy money.

To be a *visualiser* you need Art School training. However, while such training is very valuable, remember that advertisement design requires special skills which you should attempt to come to terms with as soon as possible. Some Art Schools arrange for trainees to work in agencies during vacations and this is a useful way of gaining insight. If you are not lucky enough to get this chance, read the available text books and study advertisements in the press. Above all recognise that design in advertising is a means to an end and not an end in itself. Agencies probably offer the most favourable prospect at break-in stage, but the specialist studios should not be overlooked nor such advertisers as department stores and the larger media organisations.

For those with a degree in economics, or one of the social or behavioural sciences, or who are qualified in mathematics or statistics, a career in *research* may well offer considerable job satisfaction and monetary rewards. The potential field of employment is wide and aspirants should write to companies in all branches of the business. Agencies, research companies, advertisers and media organisations all employ research personnel and there are reasonable opportunities for trainees, particularly in the bigger companies.

The basic qualities for media planning are not dissimilar, certainly in terms of a sound grasp of mathematics and/or any discipline or qualification which denotes analytical capacity. (A degree is valuable but not always mandatory.) If necessary, be prepared to tackle more general tasks at first. There are a number of assignments in the media and indeed the research area in which you can gain experience while you are waiting for the chance to receive training as a media planner.

Advertising is not a business founded on male prejudice against women. However, some areas are more favourable than others for the girl seeking a career in advertising, notably copywriting, research, media and marketing. Nevertheless, opportunities do exist in administration, particularly with agencies, companies (and publications) whose operations have an emphasis on women's interests: fashion, cosmetics, baby products, etc.

Salaries

Starting salaries for trainees depend very much on educational qualifications and the level at which entry is achieved. A graduate entering a company marketing management or big agency executive training scheme can expect to start at between £1,200–£1,500. On the other hand, a young man with 'O' levels only who may start as a production trainee in an agency can expect no more than £800–£1,000. Other starting salaries tend to range between the two extremes.

However, promotion prospects are excellent in the advertising business, given drive and intelligence, and with promotion comes commensurate rewards. A good Account Executive can expect to earn £2,000–£2,750 in his middle to late twenties, a range also applicable to an Advertising or Brand Manager. Marketing Managers and agency Account Supervisors in their early thirties may earn anything between £3,000–£4,000. Rewards for agency specialists vary: in the creative area, salaries can be higher than in account management for really talented people. In research and media planning they are marginally lower than in the executive grades but, of course, at senior management and board level they are on par with those in general administration. There are no hard and fast rules anywhere, but from the examples quoted you will see that for established personnel salaries in advertising are on the high side, higher than in some other fields. Bear in mind, however, that the figures quoted apply to 1970 and they can easily rise in subsequent years.

Courses and Qualifications

It is hoped that this book has demonstrated that advertising is no longer a 'fly-it-by-the-seat-of-the-pants-business'. Inspiration, creativity, are important, indeed they are becoming increasingly important as competition intensifies, but they must be soundly based.

Advertising is a business activity no less than any other and in all areas it requires the application of skilled judgements based upon fact and the realities of the market place. This means that young advertising personnel have to be trained on the job—and off it. The right training helps the individual not only to achieve a greater understanding of the business as a whole but also of the way the individual components contribute to and interact on one another. It also enables advertising to be related to wider business and social issues. In short, training helps to develop not only broader skills but also a professional outlook invaluable in a business which brings heavy demands and responsibilities along with high salaries.

While many employers make provision for personnel training there is clearly a need for industry training. The chief instrument for this is now the COMMUNICATION ADVERTISING AND MARKETING EDUCATION FOUNDATION (C.A.M.), established in 1969 as the result of joint action by all the leading bodies in advertising.

C.A.M.'s task is to centrally co-ordinate training and activity on behalf of the industry. Its starting point has been to tackle the urgent problem of providing facilities for beginners and those up to intermediate standard. Thus, its two-year *certificate* course, the first examinations for which were held in 1971, embraces the following subjects: a general introduction to Advertising; Business Organisation; Marketing; Market Research; Media; Copy and Design; and Production. A number of colleges in London and the Provinces have agreed to provide tuition for this course, which will also be available in *correspondence course* form.

Possession of the C.A.M. Certificate will entitle holders to sit for the C.A.M. Diploma, courses for which are scheduled to start in 1971, with the first examinations planned for 1972. Holders of H.N.C. or H.N.D. (Advertising and Marketing) are also qualified to sit for the Diploma, so there are two routes for all students. The C.A.M. Diploma has replaced the A.A. and I.P.A. Final Examinations which were held for the last time in 1971 (see note on page 144).

Diploma (i.e., final) stage study embodies more advanced tuition in marketing, market research and campaign planning, in which the student is then examined to establish whether he or she is capable of *applying* the knowledge gained. Possession of a Diploma demonstrates that the individual has been academically and vocationally trained to a high standard. The Diploma is accepted as the educational criterion for personal membership of the I.P.A. It is obviously an important factor in career advancement.

Readers who require further information about these courses and examinations should write to C.A.M., 1 Bell Yard, London, W.C.2. Those interested in *specialist* courses should also contact C.A.M., who are planning to set these up on a systematic basis. The first C.A.M. specialist course is the C.A.M. Creative Diploma, which will be offered in 1973, with the first Diplomas to be awarded in 1975.

Mention should, of course, be made of the courses and examinations sponsored by the Institute of Marketing, Moor Hall, Cookham, Berks. These embrace a very wide range of subjects, including some coverage of advertising, and constitute a valuable source of education and training for those who have chosen marketing as their career.

FOR FURTHER READING

Advertising as a Career (M. Rubin, Batsford Ltd.).

A Career in Advertising (M. Davis, Museum Press Ltd.).

Advertising (D. Thomas, Longman's Green & Co. Ltd.).

So You Think You Can Make a Career in Advertising (Advertising Association).

150 Careers in Advertising (P. Mann, Longman's Green & Co. Ltd.).

Note: All M.A.A.s and Dip. P.A.s have been replaced by the new-style Dip. C.A.M. Persons holding this qualification may join the C.A.M. Society—a society of C.A.M. Diploma-holders—and change from Dip. C.A.M. to M.C.A.M.

CHAPTER THIRTEEN

Self-Help in Advertising

So far this book has dealt with advertising in professional terms, based on the assumption that most readers are interested in pursuing a career in advertising. However, no book in this series would be complete without at least a few words of advice on 'self help' to those whose interest lies elsewhere but who would like to plan their own advertising.

CHOOSING AN ADVERTISING AGENCY

The first point is that, if such advertising is likely to be on a significant or systematic scale, the task should be entrusted to professionals, which means an advertising agency. You will have seen from this book that advertising is a highly skilled business, both in terms of planning it and organising it. This is why advertisers with small budgets as well as those with larger budgets employ an advertising agency, to take advantage of professional expertise in media planning and buying, the creation of effective advertisements and all the other services which an agency provides, from market analysis to printing.

Choosing an advertising agency is not a difficult task. The I.P.A. which represents agencies transacting more than 90% of advertising agency turnover in Britain, is always happy to advise advertisers who wish to appoint an agency. Needless to say, its advice is impartial. No professional body of the I.P.A.'s standing could afford to favour one member-agency against another. No fees are charged to advertisers seeking advice, nor are commissions levied from agencies selected as the result of I.P.A. recommendation. Thus in approaching the I.P.A. you can be sure of obtaining unbiased counsel.

This will include valuable help in establishing the kind of agency you need in regard to the level of your budget. Clearly, this is important. If your advertising budget is likely to be small, then in most cases a small agency will best suit your requirements. However, selection is contingent upon other criteria, too. If your business centres on industrial or engineering products or services, then you will probably need an industrial agency rather than one which handles mainly consumer accounts. On the other hand, if you are in mail order, an agency specialising in this kind of advertising may well be indicated, although a number of general agencies are capable of and willing to handle this type of business. 'Horses for Courses' is an old saying in racing circles and in broad terms this applies to agencies also.

It is also important to pre-determine what you want your agency to do. You may want to make extensive use of its facilities; conversely you may want only basic services. This should be made clear at the outset, since it will determine what your costs are likely to be. Contrary to popular belief, agencies work on very low profit margins (2% net profit on turnover is the average), because of high salary overheads and other costs. With larger accounts, agencies can earn their revenue mainly from commissions granted to them by media organisations. With smaller accounts, particularly in the industrial and other specialised fields, commissions are seldom high enough to yield adequate revenue for the agencies concerned. In these circumstances, a fee arrangement is negotiated and, since this is related to the work done, it is in your interests as well as the agency's to establish, as far as possible, your requirements *in advance.*

The I.P.A. publishes a leaflet called 'Choosing an Advertising Agency' which the prospective user of an agency will find very helpful.

HANDLING YOUR OWN ADVERTISING

If you decide to handle your own advertising, it is absolutely vital to approach the task in a serious and professional way. Advertising is a costly business and mistakes will make it even more so. Moreover, the penalties cannot be measured in immediate cost-terms only. By aiming your advertising at the wrong audience you not only waste your money but also neglect the right audience, and the implications of this can be far-reaching. By devising the message wrongly you can confuse, mislead, invite ridicule—and even get sued. These comments are made not to discourage you but to emphasise the necessity for getting things right, legally and ethically as well as commercially.

Defining the Problem—the Role of Advertising in Problem-solving

The first task is to analyse the problem. Let us assume you want to sell your car for ready cash. In this particular case you are in a selling rather than a trade-in situation, which suggests that it is probably advantageous to sell the car to a private buyer rather than to a dealer. In practice this usually means placing an advertisement in your local newspaper in order to expose the proposition to as many potential buyers as possible. However, before rushing out to advertise, you obviously need to fix a realistic price in relation to the make, year and condition of the car. This means that you will study the 'cars for sale' advertisements in the newspaper concerned to establish as far as possible the price-levels obtaining for similar cars under offer. Such price-levels will, of course, be influenced by seasonal factors, e.g., they are generally lower in the winter than in the summer. Only when you are satisfied you can evolve a reasonable proposition, one which meets the needs of the market-place and yet shows a satisfactory return for you, should you draft and plan your advertisement.

Note, however, that it will not sell the car by itself. All it can do is to deliver prospects. The rest is up to you—and the quality of the car in relation to price level. When prospects get in touch with you, you will need persuasiveness, a willingness and capacity to answer questions which they ask, and probably some flexibility over price. You will also have to let prospects have a test drive.

All this sounds elementary, but in fact it represents a marketing operation no less than that of the detergent manufacturers, whose advertising expenditure may total several million pounds in contrast to your £2.

The principles are the same—the bringing together of a number of elements in order to evolve a proposition which is acceptable to the buyer. Unfortunately, too many people fail to observe these principles. They invest advertising with magical qualities without realising that it is, after all, a vehicle mainly for bringing seller and buyer into contact. So they fail to do their homework; they advertise at the wrong time, they ask too high a price or they inject such hyperbole into their copy that they arouse suspicion among prospective buyers; alternatively, such hyperbole creates an expectation which is dashed when the car is inspected. Then when the car remains unsold, they are convinced that advertising doesn't work. In these circumstances, advertising becomes a scapegoat for their own deficiencies and this is all too common, in industry and commerce as well as in private transactions.

So the golden rule is to establish clearly what your problem is and how advertising can help to solve this problem. This involves understanding all the elements which contribute to the whole. It also involves understanding the advantages and limitations of advertising.

One more example to demonstrate the point. Assume now that you are the Managing Director of a small firm selling expensive industrial machinery. You are convinced that advertising can play a valuable part in helping to sell this machinery. Again, the same principles apply. You must define the problem, that is you must pin-point your market. You must ensure that your machinery meets the needs of this market in terms of price, delivery, capacity, maintenance and safety regulations.

Where advertising is concerned, it clearly cannot sell the machinery by itself. No one spends thousands of pounds after seeing a single small advertisement or even a series of them. The ultimate sale will depend upon the generous provision of information, information derived from literature and from personal contact. Indeed, demonstrations are usually necessary, with a qualified engineer in attendance to explain technicalities and the use of the machinery in relation to the needs of the prospective buyer. Thus advertising has a limited role. It cannot take the place of the salesman or the engineer. It cannot take the place of literature, given that the range of information the prospective buyer wants, which often includes quite complex specifications, can seldom be incorporated into advertisements. What it can do is to draw the attention to, or to remind prospects of, the existence of this machinery. It can highlight key benefits. It can generate requests for information, which the company can provide via literature and which it can follow up with personalised selling approaches. It can help to create *awareness* of the company, and, over a period of time, *confidence in* the company. In short, advertising can make a sizeable contribution to the ultimate sale of the machinery and to the reputation of the company. Thus it is a significant problem-solver—provided it is used to solve the right problems.

Planning your Advertising: Media Selection and Buying

In the previous section of this chapter, emphasis was given to the necessity of getting your marketing proposition right before attempting any advertising. The same point was made at greater length in Chapter 4, bearing in mind that it obtains whether your advertising is part of a sophisticated operation or merely concerned with selling a car in a local newspaper.

On the assumption that this has been done, we now turn our attention to planning advertising activity—media planning and creative execution. In Chapter 4 and again in Chapter 8, it was stressed that both elements are interrelated. Where you advertise has an influence on what you say. What you say has an influence on where you advertise.

In the earlier days of advertising it was customary to plan and book space first and to produce advertisements afterwards. This frequently meant that the advertising message had to be slotted in to fit the media requirements, both in terms of the media selected and the size of space or length of time allocated. Nowadays, it is recognised that neither activity can be planned or executed in a vacuum. Where campaign planning in an advertising agency is concerned, there is close liaison at all stages between media and creative personnel.

When you are handling your own advertising you will have to harmonise these elements yourself. In practical terms it is not difficult, since there is little likelihood that you will be involved in highly sophisticated operations which naturally call for professional team-work. The chances are that you will be concerned with newspaper, magazine or journal advertising. Therefore, the starting point is to establish media availability. *British Rate and Data* (B.R.A.D.) provides details of circulations of all press media in the U.K., together with rates, and all information which will help you to reach your decision. Sometimes, the decision is easily reached. This is when only one medium covers a given audience. In many cases, however, there are a number of media available and you have to decide which one, or which combination, you should use to reach your audience most effectively. Only the amateur would use every medium. This usually achieves unnecessary duplication and thus unnecessary cost. The rates will give you some indication of which medium or media provides the best buy in terms of costs per 1000. However, this is not the only criterion. Editorial content is also an important factor, indeed in some cases it may take precedence over pure figures. This is why you should never plan media or buy space on figures alone. Always obtain and study specimens of the media you are considering in order to get the feel of them and to establish which are creatively suitable for your proposition.

Let us take an example. There are three publications which cover retail chemists nationally:

Pharmaceutical Journal (P.J.)
Chemist & Druggist (C & D)
Retail Chemist (R.C.)

The first publication is the official journal of the Pharmaceutical Society (and by this token reaches a great many pharmacists in addition to those in the retail trade). Because of this, it is highly authoritative and, while it gives ample editorial coverage to commercial matters, its general character is professional rather than commercial. The second publication is also authoritative since it places considerable emphasis on professional matters. At the same time, however, it strongly caters for the commercial needs of the retail chemist. The last named journal is almost exclusively concerned with commercial matters. Now all three publications effectively reach most retail chemists. The choice here is contingent upon your proposition. If you are concerned with contacting all pharmacists, non-retail as well as retail, then clearly the P.J. is the natural choice. If your concern is with retail chemists only, you may consider that the choice lies between the C & D and the R.C., with the final selection turning on what kind of message you want to put over. An authoritative message clearly indicates the use of the former (although, of course, because of its official status, the P.J. should not be ruled out), whereas a strictly commercial message probably calls for the R.C.

This example demonstrates the interdependence of the media and message elements. The same thing applies to the size of the advertisement you use. It is not a matter of arbitrarily selecting a half or quarter page, or any other unit, but the determining what size of space is needed to get the message over. This, however, needs to be harmonised with the degree of frequency you think is necessary. Is it better to have four $\frac{1}{4}$ pages, or eight $\frac{1}{8}$ th pages? There is no set answer, it depends upon circumstances but if, for example, you want to achieve maximum possible frequency you will obviously go for the latter, provided you can express the proposition adequately in the smaller space. Thus media planning and basic creative planning go hand in hand.

When you have decided on the publications you will use, having achieved the coverage, frequency and size of spaces required, you are then in a position to book your space. You must, of course, allow sufficient time to get copy and blocks to the publication. (B.R.A.D. gives details of what are called *copy closing dates* for each publication), bearing in mind that some magazines want advertising material anything up to three months in advance of publication date.

In this context, booking space is not difficult, you simply contact the Advertisement Manager and negotiate with him accordingly. Do this verbally in the first instance to check on whether space is available and also on the up-to-date rate situation. When this hurdle is cleared you must then confirm your order in writing. (If you are completely unknown to the publisher, or acting on your own, you may be asked to pay for space in advance.) It is a wise precaution at the outset for the newcomer to submit proposed advertisement copy to the publication to ensure that it is acceptable and that it conforms to the British Code of Advertising Practice. One final note: if you want editorial support, do not attempt to negotiate this on the basis of the space you are buying. No reputable publication will allow its editorial policy or editorial pages to be influenced by this. It will give you editorial coverage if your story or information warrants it, regardless of whether you buy space or not. Advertising and editorial are separate entities. Keep them separate. (Although, of course, you yourself should co-ordinate your activities so that press releases are timed to coincide with your advertising effort.)

Planning your Advertising: Design and Copy

It remains for your to devise your message. Here again, you should not attempt to deal with any element in isolation. Copy and design are interrelated and should be considered together. The general practice is to rough out a design for your advertisement to the shape and dimensions of the space booked. This is not necessarily the final design but one which will give you some idea of how the basic elements—headline, copy, logotype and, where necessary, any illustrations—can be disposed. It will also give you an indication of how much space you have for copy, although if you need more space your design will have to be amended accordingly. Bear in mind that *size of type* also influences the number of words which can be fitted in to a given space. (A typesetter can provide type charts which will enable you to work this out; alternatively, you may wish to use the services of a typographer.)

When you have determined how many words you need to express the proposition you must then plan your copy, remembering the principles listed in Chapter 7. This is the selection of primary and secondary selling points, in the right sequence, backed in each case with 'reason-why' copy. This book cannot tell you how to write good copy. But it can tell you what the basic rules are:

1. *Do your homework.* This means do not be contented with superficial analysis of your proposition. If you are to find selling points which will give the reader a potent reason to buy your brand or use your service in preference to the competition, the chances are you will have to dig—and dig hard in these days of universal technical excellence. The old army maxim 'time spent on reconnaissance is never wasted' is true with a vengeance here. This is probably the hardest part of your task. You need concentration and determination to extract relevant benefits from your proposition. Remember too that the provision of relevant information is

a key benefit and to gauge such information requires considerable home-work on your part.

2. *Use simple language.* Resist the temptation to be clever and to use flip-phrases or jargon. Advertising is communication. You must communicate with your readers in language they understand. This usually means simple language. There is an old saying in advertising 'let the proposition shine clear through'. If your message is not clear at first reading, the reader will move on. You have forfeited attention and interest and, in all probability, have thrown your money down the drain.

3. *Do not be a slave to modish copy styles.* Copywriting inevitably goes through phases. One writer, somewhere, will initiate a new style to break away from the herd. Others jump on the band-wagon, and before you know where you are the new-style has become as cliché ridden and as hackneyed as that from which the original copywriter tried to break away. Avoid 'styles'. Be concerned with expressing the proposition effectively and persuasively and not with how clever you can be. The purpose of an advertisement is to influence the reader favourably, not to indulge yourself in clever word-spinning nor to impress other copy-writers.

4. *Avoid 'advertising-ese'.* All of you have probably been the victim of a speaker who uses pompous or overblown language, completely different from the language you yourself use in everyday life. Do not fall into the same trap when you write advertisements. No one in his right senses would ask for 'jet-propelled cornflakes' and is unlikely to respond favourably to a description of this type. Words like 'super', 'jumbo' and others of the same type should be avoided steadfastly. No one talks like that. No one thinks like that. Your advertisement shouldn't read like that. Use the language that your reader uses—that you use yourself when you are conversing with your fellow men.

5. *Do not confuse eccentricity with creativity.* There is an urgent need in advertising to command attention. The use of a four letter word in the headline of your advertisement would certainly achieve this but it would be the wrong sort of attention. The same is true of made-up words, zany words, nonsensical words and all the other eccentric devices which are

sometimes used by advertisers striving to be different. You have to be different, but the difference must arise from the skilful way in which you present the proposition and not from merely standing on your head.

6. *Learn to compress your arguments.* The essence of the copywriter's task is compression. In other forms of writing, you usually have time and space to amplify, even to the point of discursiveness. In advertising you have not. Every word must count if you are to hold the reader, who will quickly get bored if you are verbose or if you get bogged down.

The ability to compress, compress, compress is the thing which separates copywriting from any other form of writing. It is a harsh discipline, since the finished result must not read like a telegram. It must be succinct, lucid, persuasive and sincere—not easy requirements to fulfil in the (usually) limited space at your disposal, but essential at all times.

A Brief Note on Advertisement Production

Most commercial advertisers have advertisements made up into complete printing plates or artwork for press media. This ensures that they are identical in each publication. Moreover, it provides advertisers with plenty of scope in selecting type and evolving design and illustration. You may not be able to afford such services, although any typesetter will advise you on procedures and charges. Studios will do likewise, bearing in mind the growing use of photo-typesetting, which enables this part of the job to be executed and assembled alongside the other elements: artwork of illustrations, etc.

The extent to which you use such services depends on your budget and also the standard of advertisement design at which you are aiming. If your announcement is straightforward and simple, publications will set type for you free of charge, but remember that the range of types they have is limited and restricted to basic (but highly readable) styles. Publications will not make blocks or provide artwork free of charge, but they will advise you where you can buy such services. *Advertisers Annual* is an invaluable source of information on typesetters, studios, platemakers and all ancilliary services concerned with the translation of advertising ideas into tangible materials ready for printing and reproduction.

CHAPTER FOURTEEN

A Wider Look at Advertising

THE basic principle in advertising is to deliver the right message to the right audience at the right time at the lowest cost. This principle is universal. It obtains wherever you live. However, the environment in which advertising operates varies from country to country. So do techniques. Non-British readers of this book will obviously wish to know about the conditions and practice appropriate to their own countries. At the end of this chapter you will find a bibliography of publications issued by the I.P.A. in London, which provide valuable information on key aspects of international marketing and also on specific advertising conditions in major European countries. You will also find a list of advertising organisations throughout the Western world. Readers seeking specific data or advice about advertising in those countries should contact these organisations, the functions of which are similar to the British organisations listed in Chapter 4.

In any event, all readers, British and non-British, are advised to take an interest in advertising beyond their immediate domestic scene. This is because of the ever-growing development of commercial operations on a multi-national basis. Already many companies co-ordinate marketing and advertising activities, either globally or continentally. Among the main purposes of such co-ordination where advertising is concerned are the maintenance of a uniform corporate identity in all markets, to ensure that lessons learned in one country are applied, where relevant, in other countries, and to achieve significant cost-savings in materials over a wide range of activity.

To these ends many advertising agencies now provide services on an international basis which enable them, if required, to handle the business of their clients in any part of the world, either through subsidiaries which such agencies own in other countries or by reciprocal arrangements with domestic agencies therein. Anyone who is involved in international marketing and advertising operations quickly learns that, while there are many similarities, there are also many differences. This is because not all countries are level in terms of economic development; some are more advanced than others and this affects consumer purchasing power and spending habits accordingly, the implications of which scarcely need stressing. Social structures and cultural patterns also vary. In short, *advertising practice* (as distinct from basic principles) has to be adapted to the prevailing conditions of each country.

While these cannot be detailed, it is possible to cite a few examples in order to make the point clear. In Britain, the population is largely homogeneous, culturally as well as ethnically. This, coupled with the fact that it is contained in a small geographical unit, has led to the existence of a national press media structure which is almost unique in its capacity to provide blanket coverage of the population quickly and economically.

Such a structure is not possible in Canada. For one thing the population is not homogeneous. One third of it is French-speaking, two third. English-speaking. This obviously necessitates French and English language media, a factor which has to be taken into account when any advertising campaign is mounted, both in media planning and in creative execution. (Where the latter is concerned it also has to take cognizance of differing social and cultural attitudes.) However, even if Canada's population were homogenous, the sheer size of the country rules out national newspapers on the British pattern; moreover, there are strong regional loyalties which demand regional newspapers rather than those which are directed, as in Britain, to the entire nation.

In Holland, the press media structure is influenced by religious, political and geographical factors. With a population almost evenly divided between Protestants and Catholics, it is inevitable that some newspapers tend to be oriented one way or the other. However, there are other orientations too, to take account of strong political and geographical allegiances. Thus, although Holland is a small and compact country in which a national press structure would be feasible from a physical viewpoint, it does not possess it in the sense that Britain does.

These two examples demonstrate wide differences between countries in newspaper coverage alone and thus in media planning problems. They also underline the problems which can be encountered when devising the advertising message. Not only is it vital to communicate with each sector of a given population in its own tongue (when language differences exist as in Canada and Belgium) but it is vital also to avoid offending its ethnic, religious or political susceptibilities.

Even when no such complications arise, an advertising message capable of inducing a favourable response in one country will not necessarily be successful in another. For example, humour, particularly of the satirical type, can be and is used effectively by advertisers in Anglo-Saxon nations (U.S.A., Canada, Britain, Australia and New Zealand). However, experience has shown that this type of approach can fail dismally in certain European countries where the national temperament is different, as for example, in Germany. Non-British readers, therefore, should evaluate with care the successful advertisements featured in Chapter 7. These are successful by British standards. All are concerned with products and services which are potentially applicable to most countries in the West; however, there is no guarantee that they would be equally effective outside the U.K. in terms of *how* they express the advertising proposition.

Another area where significant differences exists is in legislation which affects advertising and sales promotion activity. This varies from country to country and all students should familiarise themselves generally with the situation which obtains in their own countries. Most countries also have some kind of voluntary control system in advertising. Again there are wide variations in the regulations imposed and the effectiveness of imposition, and these should be studied in relation to individual countries.

To summarise, therefore, differences between countries in standards of prosperity and in legislation and population and geographical characteristics prompt differences in advertising practice. At the same time, these differences should not be exaggerated. Certainly so far as Europe is concerned there are a number of fields in which it is now possible to undertake supra-national advertising, that is to say across-the-board advertising in a number of countries, with only slight individual modifications to the basic approach. In some areas of technology and business, media exist which transcend national boundaries. There are many examples, too, of the successful adaptation of American and Canadian advertising campaigns to British, Commonwealth and even European markets, and vice versa.

These and other developments indicate that points of difference between the Western nations are diminishing. This process is likely to accelerate as all become more and more committed to the consumer society and thus to a parallel outlook. The Common Market and other broad-scale trading associations, will also have their influence on the breaking down of barriers. Many people, in fact, believe that we in the Western world stand on the brink of true internationalism in commerce. If so, it is a development which offers exciting problems and opportunities for new-generation advertising men and women.

BIBLIOGRAPHY OF I.P.A. PUBLICATIONS ON INTERNATIONAL ADVERTISING

Title	Price	Format	Year
Advertising Conditions in Belgium	50p	Booklet	1971
Advertising Conditions in France	50p	Booklet	1972
Advertising Conditions in Germany	50p	Booklet	1968
Advertising Conditions in Greece	50p	Booklet	1972
Advertising Conditions in Italy	25p	Booklet	1970
Advertising Conditions in Finland	25p	Booklet	1970
Advertising Conditions in the Netherlands	50p	Booklet	1972
Advertising Conditions in the U.K.	50p	Booklet	1972
The Advertising Agency's Role in Developing International Markets	25p	Booklet	1968
British Exports—Three Myths (Treasure)		Booklet	1966
Marketing and Advertising in Europe (joint IPA/BNEC publication)		Booklet	1966
Europe means London	25p	Booklet	1972

Translating for Advertising	10p	Leaflet	1972
The Hazards of Advertising in Europe	25p	Booklet	1972
Industrial Marketing and Advertising in Europe	25p	Booklet	1970
Overseas Information Services		Leaflet	1972

OVERSEAS AGENCY ASSOCIATIONS

AUSTRALIA

Australian Association of Advertising Agencies,
408 Sussex Street,
Sydney 2000,
NSW.

AUSTRIA

Bundeskammer der Gewerblichen Wirtschaft,
Stubenring 12,
A-1010 Vienna.

BARBADOS

Advertising Agencies Association of Barbados,
c/o Corbin-Compton (Barbados) Ltd.,
Gardiner Austin's Building,
Lower Broad Street,
Bridgetown.

BELGIUM

Chambre des Agences-Conseils en Publicité,
19 Avenue E. Cambier,
1030 Brussels.

CANADA

Institute of Canadian Advertising,
Suite 401,
8 King Street East,
Toronto 1,
Ontario.

CEYLON

Advertising Agencies Association of Ceylon,
157 2/2 Dharmapala Mawatha,
P. O. Box 434,
Colombo 7.

DENMARK

Danish Association of Advertising Agencies,
7 Frederiksgade,
1265 Copenhagen K.

FINLAND

Finnish Association of Advertising Agencies,
Mainostoimistojen Liitto ry.,
P. Roobertinkatu 13B,
Helsinki.

FRANCE

Compagnie d'Agences de Publicité,
27 bis Avenue de Villiers,
Paris 17e.

WEST GERMANY

Gesellschaft Werbeagenturen,
6 Frankfurt/Main,
Friedenstrasse 11.

GREECE

Greek Advertising Agencies Association,
12 Ravine Street,
Athens 140.

HOLLAND

Vereniging voor Erkende Adverntentiebureaux,
Oosteinde 1,
Amsterdam C.

INDIA

Advertising Agencies Association of India,
111a Mahatma Gandhi Road,
Opp. Rajabhi Clock Tower,
Fort,
Bombay 1.

IRELAND

Institute of Advertising Practitioners in Ireland,
35 Upper Fitzwilliam Street,
Dublin 2.

ITALY

OTIPI,
Via Larga 19,
20122 Milan.

JAPAN

Japan Advertising Agencies Association,
Kochiwa Building,
4–8, 12 Ginza,
Chuo-ku, Tokyo.

NEW ZEALAND

Association of Accredited Advertising Agencies in New Zealand Inc.,
P. O. Box 643,
Wellington.

NIGERIA

Advertising Association of Nigeria,
c/o P. O. Box 139,
Lagos.

NORWAY

Autoriserte Reklamebyraers Forening,
Kronprinsens gt. 9,
P. O. Box 1427 vika,
Oslo 2.

SINGAPORE

The Association of Accredited Advertising Agents,
c/o Cathay Advertising Ltd.,
P. O. Box 1941,
Singapore 1.

SWEDEN

Reklambyraernas Utvecklingsinstitut AB,
Luntmakargatan 66,
P. O. Box 3160,
103 63 Stockholm 3.

SWITZERLAND

Bund Schweizerischer Reklameberater,
Seefeldstrasse 62,
8008 Zurich.

TRINIDAD

Advertising Agencies Association of Trinidad and Tobago,
c/o Corbin-Compton (Trinidad) Ltd.,
133 Oxford Street,
Port of Spain.

U.S.A.

American Association of Advertising Agencies,
200 Park Avenue,
New York,
N.Y. 10017.

Information provided by courtesy of the Institute of Practitioners in Advertising.